Motivational Teaching

# Motivational Teaching

Nick Thorner

OXFORD
UNIVERSITY PRESS

**OXFORD**
UNIVERSITY PRESS

Great Clarendon Street, Oxford, OX2 6DP, United Kingdom

Oxford University Press is a department of the University of Oxford.
It furthers the University's objective of excellence in research, scholarship,
and education by publishing worldwide. Oxford is a registered trade
mark of Oxford University Press in the UK and in certain other countries

ISBN: 978 0 19 420042 4

Printed in China

This book is printed on paper from certified and well-managed sources

ACKNOWLEDGEMENTS

*Back cover photograph*: Oxford University Press building/David Fisher

*Illustrations by*: Oxford Designers and Illustrators pp.18, 71

# Acknowledgements

I'd first like to acknowledge the work of Zoltán Dörnyei, whose many writings on motivation over the years have helped provide a great number of the theoretical insights upon which this book has been based.

I also owe a huge debt to the tireless ingenuity of the English Language Teaching community worldwide, who have revealed to me many times over what motivational teaching really looks like.

I feel especially grateful to my fellow teachers at Kings Education, Oxford, whose commitment to students and willingness to share ideas have helped incubate my own passion for teaching. In particular, I'd like to thank my colleagues Jeanette Lindsey-Clark and Nick Davids who have collaborated with me in researching motivation, not forgetting the many students who shared with us their own learning experiences during the research.

I must also recognize the heroism of my own students who, over the years, have patiently borne with me while I've experimented with both the ideas in this volume and those I buried along the way.

Sincere thanks to Andrew Dilger and Sophie Rogers at Oxford University Press for their constant support and guidance, and to Helen Gyde and Helen Wendholt for their expert editorial work.

And last but not least, I'd like to thank my dear son Jacob, who has had to entertain himself over the past few months more than any six-year-old should have to, and my lovely teenage daughter, Deyaneyra, who continues to teach me so much about motivation.

# Contents

CONTENTS

*fear of failure*
*lack of familiarity with it*
*peer learning*

*making coursebooks motivating*
*using a variety of materials*

*key features of motivating*
*tasks*

**PART 3   ISSUES IN MOTIVATION** – *81*

# Introduction

## The challenge of motivation

A passion for knowledge and learning is what draws many of us into teaching. So it can sometimes be frustrating when our students don't share this enthusiasm, especially since their futures may depend on it. Our response to this frustration helps define us as teachers. Some of us may want to confront our students about their apparent apathy. Others may feel resigned to giving help only to those who seem to want it. A more challenging approach is to recognize that there is passion and energy lurking in the classroom and attempt to draw it out through our teaching. This takes a degree of faith and optimism, and the willingness to explore the many factors that lie behind motivation.

Central to our understanding of motivation is the idea of **reward**. By 'reward' we don't mean something given to us, like a prize; rather we mean the sense of pleasure or satisfaction we get from an event, an activity, or a situation. Motivation occurs when we *anticipate* this kind of reward. Our brains release the chemical dopamine, increasing our energy levels and commitment to a task or activity. If reward is actually gained from an activity, anticipation will increase further still when we confront it again.

Though motivation seems straightforward in theory, it becomes far from simple to grasp in practice, especially when we consider a long, complex process like learning. As the focus of our thoughts shifts between tasks and situations, conflicting thoughts and emotions will compete for attention, affecting our levels of motivation. The outcomes of this battle can sometimes be surprising. For example, the desire to avoid a little displeasure in the short term (e.g. putting off exam revision) will often have a greater effect than the prospect of larger long-term rewards (like getting good results). And the desire to see others rewarded (or go unrewarded) can also motivate us regardless of the outcome for ourselves. We must also understand the many little ways in which we can feel rewarded from one moment to the next, from the simple pleasure of moving our bodies freely, to the act of relating to another human.

It is important to recognize that there are limits to how far teachers can affect motivation, particularly in the case of language learning. A great deal of progress will depend on practice done outside of class over a long time, for example. What is more, although the costs of language learning (effort, embarrassment, frustration, etc.) have to be paid out several hours a week, the pleasure of interacting confidently with users of English may not be available for some time, especially in a **first language (L1)** context. But some language teachers do inspire students, and we can certainly increase the likelihood that motivation will develop. That's where this book comes in.

## How this book is organized

Part 1 considers how we can increase students' anticipation of reward when they contemplate learning the English language, wherever they are. We'll explore the aspects of language learning they are likely to find rewarding, so the idea of learning English might appeal more (Chapter 1). We'll also look at how a focus on the future can increase positive thinking (Chapter 2), and how the acquisition process (Chapter 3) and engaging in positive learning behaviours (Chapter 4) can be made more rewarding.

In Part 2 we'll consider how we can create a more rewarding environment in the classroom so that students develop greater commitment to their courses. We'll start by considering our own behaviour as teachers (Chapter 5) and move on to explore the learning environment (Chapter 6), learner roles and responsibilities (Chapter 7), the materials we use (Chapter 8), and the way we design tasks (Chapter 9).

Finally, Part 3 considers how we can respond to background factors which can have an impact on students' motivation to learn. First, we'll address individual differences, such as gender and social roles, age, personality, and special educational needs, and see how these personal factors affect how far we anticipate reward in language learning (Chapter 10). The focus will then be broadened to look at family, culture, and learning backgrounds (Chapter 11). In the last chapter, we'll return to perhaps the most important factor, the teacher, and ask how we can inspire ourselves to motivate others (Chapter 12).

The earlier chapters in each Part address the factors that affect motivation more broadly. Subsequent chapters then deal with more specific issues. Readers may therefore find that the context provided in earlier chapters is useful when reading later ones and may benefit from reading chapters in the order in which they've been presented. However, each chapter can be read on its own, and the chapter headings are designed to guide the reader towards aspects of teaching practice that are most relevant.

The main text of the book highlights the factors behind motivation that are specific to each chapter topic, and outlines motivational pedagogic approaches that relate to them. *Try this* activities provide specific ideas and techniques that you can try immediately, while *Getting it right* sections give procedural tips to help deal with situations where motivation may be especially at risk. The *Why this works* sections at the end of each chapter provide a more academic rationale for the approaches recommended in the main text, and a starting point for further exploration of issues affecting motivation. In addition, the *Glossary* provides explanatory notes on words that appear in bold throughout the main text, and the *Useful websites* section lists online resources for extending or developing activities discussed in the book.

## Target audience

The ideas in this book are designed to suit learners from the last years of primary school to early adulthood. But all contexts vary, and the ideas are designed to provide a selection rather than a programme of action. I hope to inspire you to experiment, find solutions that work for you, and stay motivated!

# Part 1    The individual learner

# 1    A love of language learning?

Timothy Doner is a teenage hyperpolyglot, a lover of language learning. Having learnt Hebrew and Arabic at the age of just 13, he has gone on to become fluent in over 20 languages. As the motivation to learn languages comes from Timothy himself, we might describe it as **intrinsic motivation**.

It's fair to say that Timothy Doner's enthusiasm is not shared by many young people: modern languages are often rated among the least popular of school subjects. Students love the idea of being able to speak foreign languages but, unlike Timothy, they often fail to anticipate a sense of **reward** when they think about the process of learning them. On the contrary, they may expect a great deal of frustration. If we are to make English intrinsically motivating, we need to compensate for any negative feelings our students might have about it by emphasizing the aspects of language learning that are most likely to create a sense of gain and pleasure. Of course, individuals differ in what they find rewarding, so we might start by finding out what our students find pleasurable about using English.

**Try this** ☞ **A pleasure survey**

Write on the board *What is fun about English?* Invite students to think of specific things they enjoy doing in English. Write some of your own ideas to help, e.g. *watching NFL (American football) on TV, singing Justin Bieber tracks on my karaoke machine*, etc. Print images related to their ideas, such as book covers or photos of sports stars, and create a wall display.

## The pleasure of learning

Regardless of individual preferences, all learners are likely to find certain aspects of language learning particularly rewarding. When we learn a language, we not only gain an understanding of a wide range of written and spoken language forms but also an understanding of texts, from books to conversations. For many learners, these **cognitive** gains bring a keen sense of reward.

### Understanding our world

The desire to understand the language that surrounds us is a strong source of motivation. From the youngest age, we are driven to make sense of the words people around us are using. Learning a **second language (L2)** can seem less relevant in a **first language (L1)** environment, but English has become part of people's lives all over the world, and there are opportunities to explore the English around us wherever we are.

Of course, this does not mean exposing students to as much English as possible. Lack of understanding can cause displeasure, and reading or listening in L2 may create negative associations if the student believes they have understood little. Instead, we must draw attention to the English in our environment selectively.

**Try this** ☞ **Language collection**

Ask students to find objects around their homes which bear English words. They could choose packaging with English labelling (*Store in a cool, dark place.*), clothing with slogans in English (*Live the life you love!*), and so on. Ask students to research what they mean, bring them into class, and teach their peers the meaning.

## Understanding texts

Carefully exposing students to new vocabulary is particularly enjoyable: all learners feel little bursts of pleasure when the meaning of a sentence suddenly becomes clear. In fact, recent research has shown that understanding new words in context produces a similar reaction in our brains to eating good food, so we should encourage students to discover new vocabulary in every lesson. However, the sense that students have of gaining understanding of the world around them may be less great when new words come from coursebooks, even if graded texts do reduce the risk of failed understanding, so it is important to connect new vocabulary to the real world.

**Try this** ☞ **Word of the day**

Start lessons with a word of the day that has a topical relevance. For example, you could write on the board *performance* on the day of the school concert, or the word *soaking* on a wet day. Ask students to guess why you've chosen it.

**Try this** ☞ **Web connections**

We can make words from coursebooks seem more relevant by quickly searching for them online. When students query a new word in their coursebooks that can be represented visually (e.g. *escape*), enter the word into a search engine and click on the 'images' tab. Check the images are appropriate, then ask students to choose the picture that expresses the meaning of the word in the coursebook most clearly. To help them understand how useful a word is, click on the main results tab and have them record the word in their notebooks with a star rating that indicates how many search results it gets.

2bn+ (*****)

1bn–2bn (****)

500m–1bn (***)

250m–500m (**)

## Interest in language

One of the difficulties language teachers face is that their subject is often considered a tool to help describe or express ideas, like a paintbrush would be to an artist, rather than something to be learnt for its own sake. As lovers of language ourselves, we know that language can be a rich source of interest and discovery, and where possible we need to draw students into this world. We can do this by drawing attention to features of language beyond simple meanings, such as how we express politeness through language or how intonation can be used to add a further layer of meaning. As we do this, we can develop interest by asking students whether the features of English they encounter are also present in their L1.

**Try this** ☞ **Reacting to words**

When students have read a text, ask them to choose a word or two that they like, as if they are selecting chocolates. They may select a word because it has a nice sound, is used in an interesting way, or seems similar to a word in their L1. Respond enthusiastically to their ideas and make selections of your own.

**Try this** ☞ **Explore politeness**

Ask students to rewrite dialogue from the coursebook so that it has a similar meaning but is no longer polite. For example:

Good morning, can I help you? → What do you want?

Yes, I'd like some orange juice, please. → Give me some orange juice.

Sorry. There is apple juice, but no orange juice. → There isn't any orange juice. Have apple juice.

Ask them to perform the dialogue with a flat intonation to reflect the written changes they've made to the dialogue. Then see if they can put the politeness back in. Finally, discuss which version is closest to the way they talk in their L1 at home, school, or in a shop.

**Try this** ☞ **Comic onomatopoeia**

Ask students to bring in any L1 comic books they have and to find onomatopoeic words (words which sound like the thing they describe, e.g. *zoom, boom, crash, woof*). Write the English translations on the board and have students match them to their L1 equivalent. Alternatively, find some L2 comics online (by doing an image search for *comics*) and ask students to translate the onomatopoeic words into their L1. Now ask students to produce a simple comic strip of their own using onomatopoeia in each frame.

✓ *Getting it right* **Sharing understanding**

Students will get more pleasure from new understanding if they can share it. Allow each student to choose different words to look up and then share what they mean with each other.

Again, students will gain added pleasure if they can display newly acquired knowledge to other students. Posters are a particularly effective way of doing this.

**Try this** ☞    **Word posters**

Show students the poster in Figure 1.1 and explain that *nice* is an overused word, or a 'cliché'. On the board, write some words you think are overused, such as *fine, cool, happy, big, OK, said, awesome, pretty,* or invite students to suggest some. Have them choose an overused word, look it up in a thesaurus (e.g. www.oxforddictionaries. com/thesaurus), and choose ten or more synonyms. Ask them to produce their own word posters for homework and decorate the classroom with them.

FIGURE I.I     *Word poster for synonyms*

## Pleasure in language

In addition to bringing cognitive gains, working with language can bring great pleasure on an emotional level, especially when we do it with others.

### Sharing emotion

A great source of pleasure is the sharing of emotion, for example fear when watching a horror film together, or fun when we share a joke. If we can make using language a source of emotion, we may be able to make language learning seem more rewarding. We might try to provoke emotional reactions through play scripts, speeches, poems, and short stories, but there are also simpler ways that busy teachers can do this, from humorous language drills to simple games.

**Try this** ☞ **Emotion drills**

Drill words and phrases in a way that communicates their meaning. Have students say *noisy* loudly, *hungry* weakly, or *crazy* in a silly way. Then have students say the words in an opposite way, saying *crazy* in a sensible tone, for example.

**Try this** ☞ **Group storytelling**

After you've studied a set of vocabulary, divide students into groups of three. Provide them with the first sentence of a story. For example, if the vocabulary set is about furniture, start with *One day, Paolo was sitting on the sofa. Suddenly … .* Instruct the group to continue telling the story, taking turns to add a sentence with a new piece of target vocabulary.

**Try this** ☞ **Word association**

As a warmer or filler activity, have two students (A and B) sit opposite each other, with a third acting as the referee. Student A thinks of a word, then student B thinks of a word associated with it, and so on in turn. The referee decides whether the associations are strong enough.

## Special effects

Pronunciation activities are another rich source of pleasure, as they create a series of what we might consider 'special effects' of language, including rhyming and rhythm, that students tend to enjoy. Teachers of younger learners are no doubt familiar with chants, rhyming poems, and tongue twisters, but we can also create similar 'special effects' when teaching older learners.

**Try this** ☞ **Backchaining**

When teaching new vocabulary, reveal words backwards. Say the last sound and ask students to repeat it. Then add the preceding sound. Continue until the whole word has been said. Then ask students to repeat the exercise quickly without you saying the sounds. This will produce a series of rhyming effects. Using longer words like lesson subjects is particularly fun.

/i/   /dʒi/   /ədʒi/   /lədʒi/   /ɒlədʒi/   /aɪˈɒlədʒi/   /baɪˈɒlədʒi/   (biology)

The effect will be greater if students backchain at speed, as this will create a fun tongue-twister. Finally, ask students to write down the word, checking for the correct spelling.

**Try this** ☞ **Repeating to a metronome**

On the board, write some short questions of three to six syllables and some responses of the same length that you'd like students to practise. For each question/response, put a marking over the first syllable and the one that carries the main stress (shown as a high vertical mark in the following examples).

'What's your 'name?     'My name's 'Julie.

'Where are you 'from?     'I'm from 'France.

'What are you 'into?     'I'm into 'dancing.

Set a metronome (search online for *metronome*) to a slow tempo and ask students to say the exchanges to the rhythm. Allow it to be comically slow to begin with. Divide the class into two groups so one half 'converses' with the other. Gradually increase the speed of the metronome.

## Mastery

Part of the fun of doing these kinds of drills is the challenge for students of getting their lips and tongue around the sounds. Managing to do this – which we might call **mastery** – is itself a source of pleasure. Learners of music or art have the opportunity to rehearse and practise their skills to the point where they feel they've mastered them, but learners of a second language rarely enjoy similar opportunities in an L1 context, because there are fewer opportunities to practise communication. Preparing to perform chunks of texts will give learners the sense of mastery.

**Try this**  **Language performance**

After students have engaged with a listening dialogue, divide them into groups and invite each group to select a task from a set of 'performance' cards based on the dialogue script. For example:
- rap it
- perform it in the style of a silent movie (mouth words and mime)
- say numbers in place of words (to focus on stress and intonation)
- read it with an L1 accent
- read it with an exaggerated L2 accent
- personalize it by changing key words
- act it out in a certain way (e.g. using angry or affectionate voices)
- perform it with slides/special effects.

Students can select another card if they don't like their first one. Invite them to rehearse the dialogues and then perform them. Make sure that students applaud one another's performances, as mastery of a text will be all the more pleasurable if others acknowledge their achievement.

✓ *Getting it right*  **Recording performances**

Encourage students to record their performances of poems, songs, and other texts, and upload them to the school website or blog. This will gives friends and family members the opportunity to praise students.

## The senses

Another advantage of the word poster (see page 15) is that this format creates great visual impact. Young people today are used to vibrant screens and moving images, and online text is often either richly illustrated or presented in kinetic typography (animated text). Text on white pages can look comparatively dull, but homework sheets can easily be made more stimulating with different fonts and backgrounds, and within the classroom we can use colour, design, and even animated text to bring language to life.

**Try this** ☞ **Word art**

Create a graffiti wall in the classroom by covering a section of the wall with paper. Allow students to write up favourite phrases or words they have learnt (e.g. from song lyrics), encouraging them to communicate meaning through visual effects as they do so. Younger learners may enjoy doing bubble writing, whereas older ones may be able to imitate graffiti styles (see Figure 1.2). Alternatively, encourage students to record vocabulary or copy out poems on word processing software, using different fonts and text sizes. Ask them to explain their selections.

FIGURE 1.2  *Examples of bubble writing and graffiti writing*

**Try this** ☞ **Media-rich instructions**

If you have an interactive whiteboard, present instructions to the class (e.g. *Take out your homework, please.*) using the 'tickertape' function so that they move across the top of the screen, or copy them into a 'word cloud' maker (e.g. www.wordle.net) so that they appear as beautiful word clouds.

## Associations

Languages also bring learners pleasure (or displeasure) through the associations they create, and these often relate to the cultures that use certain languages. The more positive the associations learners have with a culture, the more pleasure they'll get from using its language. Many attribute the recent popularity of Spanish as a foreign language, for example, to the current popularity of Latin American culture. It is clearly very difficult to control the associations students may have formed with a language, but we can do our best to encourage them to engage with other cultures.

**Try this** ☞ **Cultural engagement**

If you come across a cultural reference in the students' coursebook, encourage them to research it further online. For example, they could find out what a person mentioned in one of their coursebook texts is doing now (check they are real people first), or they could add new details to a description of a place or a festival they have read about.

The English language is no longer just associated with national cultures but is also gaining exciting new associations with vibrant online communities, for example of gamers or music fans. Encouraging students to get involved with online communities could also help them develop positive associations with English. A student who gets 500 'likes' from English speakers for a blogpost they've written is likely to consider learning English very rewarding.

However, it is vital that teachers are aware that the greater exposure students have online, the greater their risk of internet abuse. In fact, teachers can't actively encourage students to share files on public forums because most file-sharing websites (e.g. YouTube) won't allow them to have an account until they are 18 (13 with permission from a parent/carer). Yet asking older students only to use intranets or closely monitored virtual learning environments won't help to increase their motivation.

*online*

One way of dealing with this dilemma is to give older students confidence to engage with online communities safely, and to teach them how to produce great content so that they will have positive experiences of online communities when they're ready to join them.

✓ *Getting it right*

**E-safety**

Ensure students have proper e-safety training before uploading content to any online environment. Areas you could cover include the 'Grandma rule' (don't post what you wouldn't want Grandma to see), reporting and blocking abusive users, using 'restricted mode' (with filters), disabling and removing the 'comments' function, responding to personal messages cautiously, and using 'private' and 'unlisted' options when posting videos.

**Try this** ☞

**Video tutorials**

Ask students to produce a video tutorial related to lessons. It could be about how to illustrate their lesson notes, or how to learn a new word so they will never forget it. Get students to edit their videos with an app on their mobile devices (if they are allowed to use them in class) such as iMovie (for iOS) or VideoShowLab (for Android). They could speed them up so that they are fun to watch, and add a music track using VideoFX or a similar app.

Help them to record a short introduction, e.g. *Hi, guys. My name's ... and I'm going to show you how to ... . I hope you enjoy it. Don't forget to 'like' it!*

Have students upload their videos to the school's internal file-sharing system, and review each other's videos.

**Why this works** ⫸

**Intrinsic motivation**

Intrinsic motivation has been discussed since the 1970s and is considered the most effective form of motivation, since it results in long-lasting and self-sustaining effort. In a language-learning setting, the term can also be used to describe students' willingness to engage with any activities without a reward being offered. In this chapter, however, we have discussed a part of intrinsic motivation that is particularly elusive, namely an interest in foreign languages itself. This aspect of intrinsic motivation is even more valuable because it may motivate students to engage with language study when they leave the classroom.

# 2            Reflecting on the future

Most teachers would probably like their students to think about their futures a little more often. If learners knew what they wanted to be doing in five or ten years' time, they'd see the purpose behind their schoolwork and be motivated to study. This kind of motivation is often called **instrumental motivation**, and the more a student reflects on their ambitions and associates them with the task ahead, the stronger this motivation will be.

## The ideal future self

Reflecting on the future has an additional benefit. Young people usually imagine their future self as being a more powerful and successful version of their current self. So, just as reflecting on past mistakes can make learners feel negative, reflecting on potential growth can help them develop a positive self-image. This in turn will increase their expectation of themselves and raise motivation. In other words, their future self will act as a positive reference point, or a behavioural guide.

For learners of English, the possible future self is a particularly attractive one. The prospect of accessing global conversations and culture can plant exciting ideas in their minds about the people they might become. However, the present has such a strong hold on us that we sometimes lose sight of the place we want to get to or the person we feel we can be. Encouraging young people to reflect on their aims and their future lives can restore this future focus and the motivational benefits that come with it. It's a good idea to explore students' current motivations to learn English in order to raise awareness of the need for a **future self-guide**.

**Try this** ☞ **Reflect on motivation**

Ask students to work in groups and discuss why they are there in the classroom learning English. Allow them to work in their L1. You might hear ideas such as the following:

> We have to learn it in this school.
> I want to understand what people are saying online.
> I'll need it for the job I want to do.

Write their reasons on the board in two categories. On the left put ideas connected with their current lives, and on the right those connected with their future lives. If some reasons could relate to both (e.g. the second reason above), ask students to clarify. Now add the column headings *My life now* and *My future*.

Ask students which column has more reasons and why. Then ask which reasons they think are more exciting or important.

✓ *Getting it right*

### Feedback

Use your feedback to students to encourage them to reflect on their futures. Phrases such as *You won't need my help soon* will give them the sense that they are moving towards a target state. Where possible, refer to their future ambitions too, e.g. *It won't be long before you're presenting in English!* This approach also helps to make feedback highly specific, but be sure to only say things you believe are possible.

Students can best develop positive views of themselves as language users by considering the many benefits that English may bring them. Websites that sell English language courses are a good source of ideas.

**Try this** ☞

### Research the benefits

Give students a worksheet similar to the one in Figure 2.1, entitled *Reasons to learn English,* with 6–10 shapes or spaces to write reasons in. Tell them to type the worksheet title into a search engine, either during class or for homework, and to open some of the links. If necessary, students can use an L1 translation of the worksheet title, or translate English pages into their L1 by copying web addresses into Google Translate.

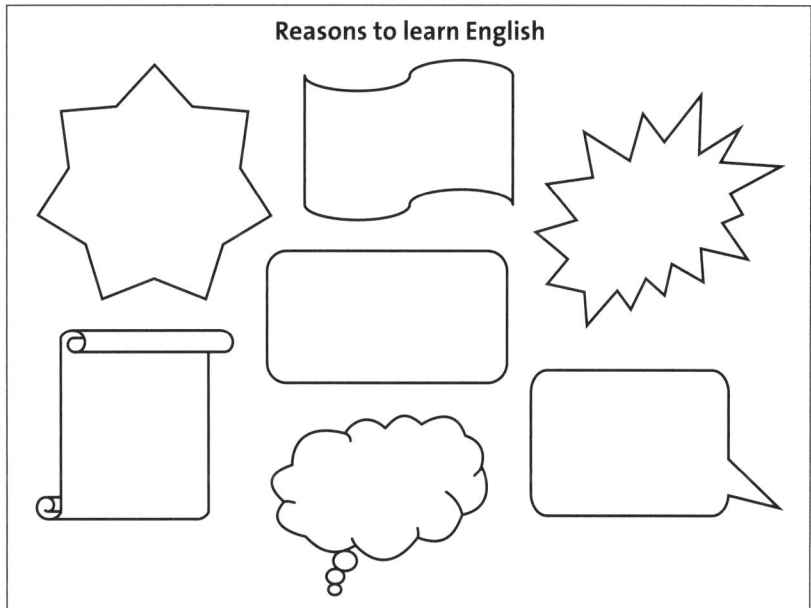

FIGURE 2.1  *Worksheet for benefits of learning English*

Then put students in groups to share their ideas. Have each group agree on their five most exciting reasons and write up their ideas on the board. Students can then make a class poster or display of the most popular ideas.

Students may end up with a list of benefits similar to the following, taken from real advertising for English language schools:

a   earn more money than your peers
b   read 95% of academic research
c   work in science, technology, or business
d   watch foreign TV networks
e   go to an international conference
f   work in an international organization
g   understand emergency instructions on planes, etc.
h   impress your friends and family, just by speaking
i   chat with 2.5 billion people.

Such lists are selling us nothing less than a vision of our future. The websites and adverts where they are found use imagery and narratives to make these visions even more powerful. Could we also use the vehicle of advertising to sell English to students? If it's true that salespeople end up believing their own sales talk, imagine what might happen if we turned students into advertisers of English. Alternatively, to help students develop a more personal, detailed view of the future, we could encourage them to reflect on a typical day in their future as an English speaker.

**Try this** ☞   **Adverts for English**

Have students bring in printed adverts and ask them to identify what they are promising. For example, an advert for trainers may imply that their owners will gain sporting success. Then ask students what they would promise a buyer if they were selling English lessons to them. Have them create an advert for English lessons, using images cut out from the adverts they brought in, or compiling digital images on computers. Students then vote for the most persuasive advert.

**Try this** ☞   **Future diary 1**

Ask students to write about a typical day in their future. Start by getting them to choose five things they'd love to be able to do one day using English. Show them the list of benefits above to help them. Then give them the example of a future diary entry below. Have students identify which five items on the list the author of this diary entry chose (c, d, e, f, and i). Students then write their own future diary entry including five ideas of their own.

*My typical day (ten years in the future)*

*It had been a difficult day. I had attended a conference in Chicago with 50 computer game designers from around the world. The presentation I'd given for my company was a success, but as I sat in my hotel and caught up with the news on CNN I felt tired. Then the phone rang. I picked it up and responded in English, but it was only my mum. 'Is that really you, Gianni?' she asked. 'Wow, your English accent is so good!' After she'd hung up, I felt better and I decided to go down to the bar. I got chatting to a group of interesting people working with a modelling agency, and we decided to head out to see a film at the local English language cinema. It was a great evening.*

✓ *Getting it right*

**Encouraging imaginative thinking**

If you have lower-level students, consider doing imaginative thinking activities in their L1 first. The objective is to engage students in free, imaginative thinking, and having to use their L2 may impede this process. Such activities could be followed up with a translation task in which students express their ideas in English.

Children of primary school age will probably feel comfortable talking about what they're going to be 'when they grow up', but a class of teenagers may feel a little self-conscious about revealing their inner ambitions. For older classes, teachers could take a less direct approach, by encouraging students to identify with other young people who have become proficient in English. While teachers rarely have the opportunity to introduce students to an L2 speaker who can be a **role model**, the internet can be a useful source. For example, video logs (vlogs) on YouTube regularly feature non-native speakers posting videos of themselves speaking in English.

**Try this**

**Language role models**

Have students profile a user of English that they admire from their own L1 background. They might profile a vlogger (or YouTuber) from their country, for example, giving details of where they work, what they vlog about, the languages they use, how many subscribers they have, their most popular vlog, a quote, etc. Alternatively, they could investigate a family member or a friend, discovering how and when they became proficient in English, and how they use English now. They could record an interview with them and share it with the class.

✓ *Getting it right*

**Identifying with students**

If you're a non-native speaker of English, using yourself as a role model can be a good way of helping your students to identify with you, and to believe that success is possible. Talk about what you were and weren't able to do in English at their age, focusing on things that they do better than you could.

# The 'ought to' self

So far, we have focused on how learners can reflect on the person <u>they</u> want to become, but social and cultural expectations can also influence who we think we *ought to* be. For example, a student may want to avoid disappointing other people, particularly family members. In other words, they may be motivated to become their **'ought to' self**, not from embracing a positive view of themselves but from fear that they may be a lesser person than others expect.

As teachers, we do not wish to create a sense of fear or anxiety in our students, but we should be open to using the 'ought to' self as a source of motivation. A focus on imaginary social encounters may help strike the right balance.

**Try this** ☞ **Future diary 2**

Adapt the future diary 1 activity (see page 22) by asking students to write a mirror image of the first diary entry, in which they don't speak English well. For example:

> *I was returning home after a meeting with colleagues at the small, local company where I worked. I was exhausted after a long and boring day. While I was waiting at the bus stop, a young Australian tourist approached me and asked if I knew of a local bar. I knew what they were asking but couldn't find the words to respond. 'Sorry, no help' was all I could say in English. Disappointed, the tourist walked off … .*

You could then make a copy of these and ask students to ceremoniously throw the copies in the bin!

✔ *Getting it right* **Managing anxiety**

Be careful not to add to any pressure that students may already feel to meet social and cultural expectations. Discussion of the 'ought to' self should be about exploring existing pressures rather than adding new ones, and should be light-hearted and humorous in nature.

The desire to avoid social embarrassment is another dimension of the 'ought to' self that should be possible to discuss quite safely. There are a variety of adverts that can be used to explore this idea in a light-hearted way. Search on YouTube for *Should've gone to Specsavers* to bring up a list of adverts for an optician's, in which people's eyesight has failed them with humorous effects. For example, there is one involving a shepherd who shears his sheepdog, mistaking it for a sheep.

**Try this** ☞ **Should've learnt more English**

Show students a 'Should've gone to Specsavers' advert and have them translate the strapline into their own language. Explain that you'd like them to create an advert for learning English, with the strapline *Should've learnt more English*, in which something unfortunate happens because someone doesn't know enough English. To illustrate, show or draw the following signs and ask students to decide what might happen if someone didn't understand them:
- Stand on the right (on an escalator)
- Push/Pull (on a door)
- Formal dress (on an invitation)
- Do not disturb (on a door)
- Warning: guard dog (on a gate)

Give them time to prepare their adverts, encouraging them to include simple dialogues in speech bubbles.

Another approach to exploring the 'ought to' self is to look at our future selves from a different perspective. One way to gain this perspective is to imagine comments that people might make about us in the future. This is a trick that has been used by motivation guru Daniel Pink in his *One Sentence Project*, a very simple but wonderfully effective idea.

**Try this** ☞ **One sentence project**

Find a YouTube video of the *One Sentence Project* showing young people reading sentences in the third person, such as *He was a very patient father*. Ask who the young people might have been talking about (themselves from a future viewpoint). Then ask students to imagine what they'd like others to say about them in the future. Here are some examples:

> He always helped others.
> Her ideas helped change the world.
> She flew with her own wings.
> She saved many lives.
> He made people laugh.

Correct their sentences if necessary, then video the class as they say them and upload the video to the school website or blog if you have parents'/carers' permission. Then ask them to discuss how English can help them become that person.

# The present self

It can be very difficult to keep our future self-guides in mind when confronted with day-to-day realities that seem to contradict them. In particular, our present level of attainment can weaken the belief we have in our ideal future self. Teachers therefore need to find a way of connecting students' current views of themselves with their idealized views. One way to do this is to help them visualize the journey towards their ideal and encourage them to imagine *how* they are going to arrive at their destination.

**Try this** ☞ **A success story**

Ask your students to choose one thing they would like to be able to do with English. It could be a wild ambition, such as publishing a novel in English, or a more concrete one, such as entering university. Write up these questions and ask them to make notes.

> What progress have you already made?
> What exactly will need to happen to help you achieve the goal?
> How will you feel when you have achieved it?
> How will your life change as a result?

Then tell students to imagine they have achieved their goal and an article about them is appearing in the newspaper. Ask them to write a newspaper headline about their success, five years in the future, e.g. *Boy, 18, publishes first novel in English*. Then have students write an article for the headline, explaining how the achievement happened. Encourage them to share ideas on how to make their stories more realistic.

A moment of weakness or laziness in the present may also encourage us to believe that our stronger future self is an illusion. It's therefore important that teachers try to stop students falling into habits that will cause them to lose sight of their future self-guides. Very often this will mean encouraging them to give up current pleasures in the interest of greater pleasure in the future, which in psychological terms is called **delaying gratification**. This temporary sacrifice is easier when witnessed by others, and so reflecting on it can be a useful class activity. We could even reflect on how our future self might view our sacrifices.

**Try this** ☞ **'Thank you' from the future**

Ask students what they would prefer to be doing now rather than being in class. They might suggest playing football or video games. Now have them write a thank-you letter from their future self to their present self, thanking them for their sacrifice. Have students read each other's letters.

## Reinforcing future self-guides

A further potential barrier to helping students embrace their future self will be the lack of teaching time available. Teachers can't dedicate hours of class time to strengthening students' images of their future. We must therefore find ways to create reminders of these future selves. We could also take steps to link the future orientation theme with something students see regularly, such as wall space or coursebooks.

**Try this** ☞ **Constant reminders**

Display any letters, future-self stories, and 'ought to' posters that students create. Wall displays could be created under inspiring headings such as *Our future has begun!* or students could keep letters from their future selves inside their exercise books.

**Try this** ☞ **Personalizing the contents page**

Have students discuss what they want to do with English (e.g. socialize, follow instructions, travel, etc.); they may be able to draw on ideas included in the future diary 1 activity (see page 22). Write their ideas on the board, then ask them to look at the contents page of their coursebook and identify pages or lessons that they think will be most useful to them. Encourage them to circle those references on the contents page or label them with smiley faces. This will help students build up a picture of how the programme of study will contribute to their visions. Note students' choices and, when you teach a lesson that they have expressed a particular interest in, invite them to contribute a personal lesson objective or suggest how the material might be tailored more to their needs and expectations.

**Why this works** ▌▌▌➡

> ### Reflect on the future self
>
> The image of oneself as a proficient L2 speaker is often referred to as 'the ideal L2 self'. Focusing on the future self is a simple idea, but one that draws together several of the important ideas in motivation theory that involve long-term purpose or ideals:
>
> - belief that English will help us achieve something (instrumental motivation)
> - desire to belong to a community of language users (**integrative motivation**)
> - an increase in our assessment of personal value (**self-worth**)
> - an ability to keep sight of personal aims (**self-regulation**).
>
> Researchers suggest that reflecting on the future self will be most motivating if we also consider the 'nightmare' future too, in which we fail to achieve learning objectives.
>
> Zoltán Dörnyei, a proponent of the future-self idea, and Jill Hadfield have developed a teaching programme to help develop this future orientation in students, including visualization techniques to help them reflect on their future (see *Useful Websites* for Zoltán Dörnyei's website). However, simple activities with outputs that can be viewed repeatedly will also be of benefit.

# 3        Seeing progress

In the previous chapter we discussed the importance of having a dream to aspire to, but we have to enjoy the <u>process</u> of achieving our dreams if we are going to work for them. Let's reflect on doing a jigsaw puzzle, for example. If we simply wanted the picture, we wouldn't spend hours putting the pieces together – we'd buy a poster! It's the pleasure of taking the small steps *towards* completing it that makes us maintain our commitment. Unfortunately, progress in language learning is not as steady and manageable as it is for jigsaw enthusiasts, but it is the teacher's job to make it as similar as possible.

## Setting goals

We can introduce a regular sense of achievement by breaking down the language-learning process into a series of goals. If the goals are discussed and agreed, they become more valuable, since others can witness a learner's achievements, increasing their pleasure in learning. The agreement also adds a sense of obligation, appealing to the 'ought to' self, discussed in Chapter 2. Furthermore, if goals are arranged in a planned sequence, learners gain a sense of progression as they achieve them.

But what should the goals be? A common type are **performance goals**, where learners attempt to demonstrate their ability to perform at a certain standard, usually by passing an external assessment like those offered by Cambridge English. These assessments are often motivating because they are widely valued, and the perceived **value** of a goal increases motivation.

However, performance goals are regularly criticized. Firstly, students may only be encouraged to work on them when assessments draw near. Also, motivation may drop if learners fail to achieve a certain level or, equally, when they manage to do so. Note that using a programme of regular tests such as the Trinity GESE suite can help limit these problems by ensuring that success or failure is followed by a fresh challenge or opportunity. Finally, performance goals can lead to students comparing themselves to each other if given indiscriminately to all class members, which may demotivate weaker students. Allowing students to 'opt in' to tests where possible, or setting different performance goals for each student, may prevent this happening.

## ✓ Getting it right

**Optional testing**

Offer external tests to students periodically (if your school allows this), but avoid making them compulsory. Instead, encourage demotivated students to participate by saying you believe they can do well (if that is the case), and let others sign up if they want to. Inviting students to take the exam on an individual basis will prevent class members making comparisons.

An alternative approach is to use competence-based assessment, where students aim to acquire specific skills rather than reach a certain level of performance. These skills are often called **learning goals** and may take the form of a list of 'can-do' statements that students tick off. The statements can also be tied to external systems of validation. The Council of Europe, for example, provides a very specific list in the document entitled *Common European Framework of Reference for Languages: Learning, Teaching, Assessment* (often shortened to 'CEFR'). Here is an example of one sublist of competences for speaking:

---

**Sustained monologue: Describing experience (A2)**

Can tell a story or describe something in a simple list of points.

Can describe everyday aspects of his/her environment, e.g. people, places, a job or study experience.

Can give short, basic descriptions of events and activities.

Can describe plans and arrangements, habits and routines, past activities and personal experiences.

Can use simple descriptive language to make brief statements about and compare objects and possessions.

Can explain what he/she likes or dislikes about something.

www.coe.int/lang-CEFR

---

TEXT 3.1  *Speaking competences for A2*

---

**Try this** ☞ **Learning goals**

Provide each student with a list of learning goals for the CEFR level matching your syllabus. Store the lists in the classroom and take them out periodically, asking students to tick off writing, reading, and listening competences based on 'pass' grades you have awarded for related skills assignments. For speaking, ask them to record specific tasks and to listen back to their recordings. Invite them, or a partner, to decide if their performance meets the 'can-do' criteria or if they should try again.

With younger learners, competence lists can be adapted around simple topics that the learners can identify with more easily, such as 'my school' or 'the weather'. For example, the descriptor *Can describe everyday aspects of his/her environment* might become *I can describe my classroom* and appear under the heading 'My School'. Many schools in Europe combine this with biographical information in a document known as a European Language Portfolio.

✓ *Getting it right*   **Strategies for achievement**

Make sure all goals are accompanied by strategies for achieving them, even if they seem like simple tasks. Do this by adding the word 'effectively' to a learning goal and providing three simple strategies for students to bear in mind:

**I'm going to describe an event effectively, by:**
- using the past simple tense
- using sequence adverbs, such as *next*
- saying what I liked/disliked about it.

This will motivate students because they will then know how to achieve success.

## Short-term goals

Goals stir us into action more quickly if they are short term. It is also easier for learners to imagine how they will achieve smaller, short-term goals which, in turn, increases their **expectancy** of achievement.

Learning vocabulary provides a particularly rich opportunity for short-term goal setting, and many teachers can set targets such as 'one word a day'. Most vocabulary items have been classified at CEFR levels (go to www.englishprofile.org), so students can have the satisfaction of knowing that their word knowledge is helping them achieve certain standards.

**Try this** ☞   **Target word labels**

In each lesson, have students select a word or phrase from their coursebooks that they'd like to use outside class, and write it on a sticky label. For example:

> I'm gonna say
>
> **Lucky you!**
>
> today

Ask them to stick the label on something they bring to school every day, and to remove it only once they have used the word/phrase outside of class. In the next lesson, check who has removed their label and ask them to explain how they used the word/phrase. Students could collect 'used' label in their exercise books.

**Try this** ☞   **Avoiding clichés**

Ask students to make a list of clichés that they should avoid in speaking or writing (e.g. *nice*), or put up posters with 'banned' clichés on the walls. Reward students with praise when they use an appropriate alternative.

We should also note that regular attempts at *achieving* goals help learners to stay committed to the task, since they can experiment with new strategies if they are unsuccessful the first time. The ability to attempt a new 'high score' in a game, for example, can make the activity quite addictive.

**✓ *Getting it right*** | **High scores**

If students are allowed to use mobile devices in class, let them play language learning games with high score features (*English Vocabulary Builder* from Miracle FunBox is a good example) at the end of lessons when they've worked well, or encourage them to play the games outside of class. Ask them, from time to time, if they've beaten their high scores.

Successfully memorizing a word, or realizing that we've started to use a word that was once new to us, can be very rewarding. Unfortunately, many students fail to embrace this opportunity for pleasure, perhaps because they don't record words in a way that makes self-testing possible, or because the prospect of memorizing a word before being able to use it isn't very appealing.

**Try this ☞** | **Word cards**

Ask students to make a set of word cards that can be used to test vocabulary. On one side, they write the word, the word stress and pronunciation, and the part of speech, e.g. noun, verb, etc. On the other side, older students can write a definition while younger students can draw a picture. Online tools such as those at https://quizlet.com can be used to make digital word cards.

**✓ *Getting it right*** | **Self-testing**

Make sure you give students the support they need to help them record new words appropriately. Set aside class time to do this and for self-testing.

Memorizing a boxful of word cards or a long list of vocabulary, however, can be a daunting prospect. Students need to feel that they are gaining mastery over the words and committing them to memory. Marking words as 'learnt' in some way will give them a sense of control and progress. Older students might do this by ticking or highlighting words, while younger students may prefer colouring.

**Try this ☞** | **Word pictures**

Ask younger students to write new words into segments of a picture that you've provided, e.g. bricks in a picture of a castle or leaves on a tree. When a student has made progress by demonstrating that they have learnt one of these words, allow them to colour in the segment for this word. For example, you might require them to recall the words successfully in a test, identify them in a storybook you're reading to them, or use them in a sentence.

**✓ *Getting it right*** | **Recording learnt words**

Learners are often a little too ready to declare words 'learnt', so design systems that allow them to return to old words. They could write vocabulary on word cards that they can move from a 'new word' box to a 'learnt' box and back, if necessary. Alternatively, a simple system for showing how well they've learnt words (e.g. *one tick = I can recall it accurately, two ticks = I'm using it*) will help them think carefully before ticking.

## Difficulty

A final point to consider when setting goals is difficulty. Goals are more motivating when they represent a challenge, even if some students respond to challenge more than others. If students simply progress from one competence to the next or one word to another within a given proficiency band, they may not get a sense of growing accomplishment. However, with grammar learning especially, it is possible to structure even short-term goals to reflect rising degrees of challenge.

**Try this**     **Degrees of challenge**

Set students a sequence of goals for each language structure you teach and assess whether they've reached each one. Use the following seven stages. (Examples of how students might achieve each goal have been added for the present perfect structure in *I've never drunk tea*.)

1 Order the words (~~never I have drunk~~ *I've never ...*)
2 Produce forms accurately (~~I am never drink tea~~ *I've ...*)
3 Make substitutions to change meaning (*I've always preferred coffee.*)
4 Recognize it (in the coursebook, in conversation)
5 Identify opportunities to use it (in response to the question *Do you like tea?*)
6 Pronounce it naturally (put stress on *never* and *tea*)
7 Change meaning with stress and intonation (shift stress to *I* or *drunk*)

✓ *Getting it right*    **Stretching students**

Encourage students to select their own aims from a sequence like the one above. As you monitor them, draw their attention to where they are in the sequence and encourage them to aim for the next stage.

## Progress orientation

The idea of constantly aiming for small, measurable improvements needn't only apply to goal setting. It can also be part of a general orientation of lessons to help students notice progress. The strict grading of language that we find in some courses can seem frustrating for students who want to see rapid skills development. The freedom to learn more challenging language can restore a sense of control and interest. It may also allow them to acquire language that they feel might impress others.

✓ *Getting it right*    **Advanced language**

If students notice language above their level, perhaps as they listen to a song or watch a film, don't discourage them from learning it – especially chunks of language that can be memorized simply, such as *You've gotta be joking*. Tell students that it's a higher level of English, but that you think they should try it out!

Teachers might then try to break away from the staged development of language over long cycles in favour of a more vertical progression, as illustrated in Figure 3.2, in which learners extend simple structures they already know.

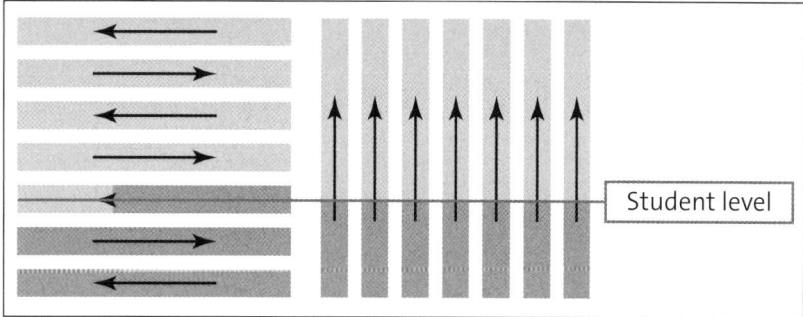

FIGURE 3.2    *Staged and vertical language development*

In this approach, the role of the teacher becomes one of guiding or mentoring students to help them achieve greater impact with their words. The emphasis on improving text can either be adopted through separate activities or integrated with the coursebook, as the following activities illustrate.

**Try this** ☞    **Skeleton writing texts**

Tell the class to imagine they are writing a postcard. Write up a few basic sentences, inviting them to contribute details such as who they are writing to, where they are, etc.

> *Hi Paul,*
> *I am writing to you in a café in Paris. I am drinking some juice. Paris is lovely. You can visit lots of galleries ... .*

Now invite students to discuss in groups what they can add to improve the text (adjectives, adverbs, conjunctions, etc.) and invite groups to come to the board and make changes in turn.

> *I'm writing to you in a **delightful** café in **the centre of** Paris, **where** I'm **happily** drinking some **peach** juice. **This city** is **so** lovely and you can visit a lot of **interesting** galleries ... .*

Provide another skeleton text for students to rewrite in pairs or groups.

**Try this** ☞    **Language makeover**

When you next come across a language 'function' in a coursebook (e.g. 'apologizing'), elicit vocabulary and phrases that students already know (*I'm sorry*) and write them on the board. Then extend or improve the sentence, using ideas from the coursebook and students' wider knowledge. You could elicit words and phrases that they might use in their own language and ask them to translate the words and phrases using Google Translate. They could try strengthening the meaning (*I'm so sorry*), extending the phrase (*I'm so sorry for hurting you*), or adding a phrase (*I'm sorry, I didn't mean to*). Deal with additions as lexical chunks rather than teaching the grammar.

This orientation towards progress can be strengthened by setting objectives for every piece of work a student does.

 *Getting it right*    **Language objectives**

Make sure every piece of written work is accompanied by clear, achievable language objectives; for example, ask students to include five adjectives. You could also set a *negative* objective to avoid a particular typical mistake. This will provide you with something positive to say about your students' language progress each time they complete a piece of written work.

## Owning progress

Students will gain a greater sense of progress if we give them regular opportunities to improve their work and demonstrate improvement. Learners can best do this through ongoing projects or collections of work that they can access whenever they like, and show to their parents/carers or peers. This is one of the ideas behind the **learning portfolio**.

**Try this** ☞   **Learning portfolios**

Have students store their work in a folder or in a shared online area, where they can update it as often as they like. They might add a diary or blog explaining what they were trying to achieve with each piece of work. For example, if they've recorded themselves giving directions, they could write about how they were trying to use the imperative or prepositions of place, and identify the CEFR 'can-do' statement they've achieved.

Allowing students to keep self-assessment tools with them, such as the list of CEFR 'can-do' statements, will also give them control over when and how frequently they *assess* their progress. The seven stages of learning a grammar structure, discussed on page 32, could also be turned into a self-assessment tool.

**Try this** ☞   **Achievement ladder**

Give each student a copy of an 'achievement ladder' grid (see Figure 3.3) to keep in the back of their exercise books. The grammar structures along the bottom row should be the structures you plan to teach over the coming term. Allow students to colour in or tick the relevant boxes on the grid whenever they feel they have achieved the level of ability indicated on the ladder to the left.

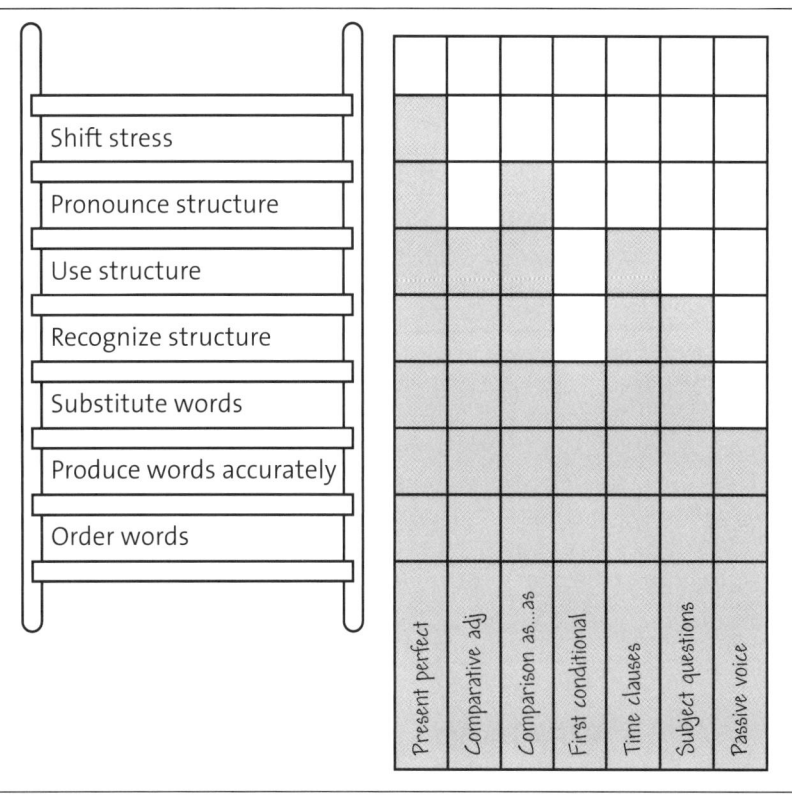

FIGURE 3.3   *Achievement ladder for different grammar structures*

Keeping portfolios and self-assessment sheets allows students to look back and reflect more regularly on their achievements. Reflecting on past effort in particular can make people more committed to learning and underline the fact that the progress they make in performance assessments is the product of hard work, reinforcing the idea that their actions bring results. Finally, to emphasize that students are responsible for their achievements, we should not only note their progress but also congratulate them on it.

**Try this** ☞   **Unit certificates**

As you finish each unit or module, ask students to complete a certificate for themselves. This could encourage them to reflect on vocabulary, functions, and other skills they've acquired. Make templates available on the school intranet or print out blank certificates. Then students can do the following: compare their certificates; photograph them and share them on social media pages; upload them to online portfolios or profiles; or display them on walls.

Module _3_ certificate

Between _11–28 September_

The student _Elena Gomez_ of class 4A

discovered the new words

_hill, field_

and used them when she

_wrote about the countryside._

She also learnt information about

_rainforests_ in English

and how we _buy train tickets_

in English.

FIGURE 3.4 *Example unit certificate*

## ✓ *Getting it right*

**Assessment parties**

When students are ticking off competences or looking back through portfolios, create a party atmosphere with music or refreshments, for example. Reinforce student achievement by offering a class reward, such as the opportunity to choose a song or watch a video clip.

**Why this works** ⅢⅢ➤

**Recording progress**

Seeing progress towards goals is essential because it gives learners a sense of **self-efficacy** – the belief in their potential to achieve. This will raise their expectation of achievement and bring pleasure to the learning experience itself, motivating further study. Seeing progress is particularly important for those learning a skill because it can be difficult to notice general improvements in skills performance. Learners often report having reached a 'plateau' in their development, despite their efforts. Tools that help them notice little improvements can therefore provide much-needed reassurance. Self-efficacy will be stronger still if learners are able to attribute their successes to their own efforts, through keeping records of work and progress.

The effects of goal challenge and of short-term (proximal) goals can be read about in the research of Edwin Locke & Gary Latham, and of Albert Bandura, respectively. For information about performance vs learning goals, read the work of Carol Dweck (see *Useful websites* section).

# 4 Motivating specific behaviours

When we say our students are unmotivated, what we usually mean is that they are not motivated to engage in learning behaviour. If we asked them to play football or chat with friends, motivation may reappear. In fact, they may also be *generally* willing to engage in learning behaviour, but just not *now*. There is a big difference between making students disposed to learning English and getting them to do it right away. So, in addition to motivating our students to learn English, we need to think about how to bring students to the 'action' stage of learning. To do this, we must be clear about the kind of behaviour we want students to engage in.

## Learner behaviour

### Awareness

Students need to know which actions and activities will help them learn before they can motivate themselves to perform them. This may be an obvious point, but some students might have the impression that simply turning up to class or copying a friend's answers into their exercise books is an adequate learning strategy. It's therefore worth exploring good learning habits as a class activity.

**Try this** ☞ **Learning habits**

Tell learners that being an effective learner will require them to <u>think</u> in a certain way, <u>do</u> certain things, and <u>engage</u> regularly with other people. Draw three circles and ask them to think of things for each category that language learners must do. See Figure 4.1 for an example.

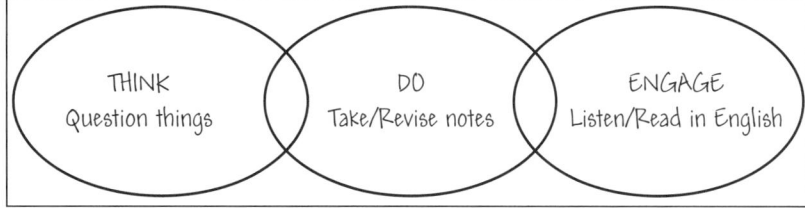

FIGURE 4.1  *Example diagram of different learning habits*

**Try this**    **Target behaviour posters**

You can use a list of good learning habits for a further activity. Have students think of some 'opposite' behaviours (e.g. remain silent, ignore new words) and design a 'Learning English Dos and Don'ts' poster. Encourage them to order behaviours with the most important first.

✓ *Getting it right*   **Owning behaviour**

Asking students to produce a list of good behaviours themselves will prevent it from seeming like a list of classroom rules. This is essential because we are far more likely to engage in behaviours that we have thought of ourselves.

## Tools for learning

Many learning behaviours can be supported by the use of physical objects. Objects that we can put in front of us, pick up, and use may attract our attention more easily than instructions or guidance on walls, and may remind us to practise the good behaviour associated with it. Secondly, having certain tools available can make some behaviour more likely. For example, students often avoid checking work because they dislike spoiling their neat writing with corrections, so correction pens or erasers and soft pencils can promote this behaviour.

Young people also love to use different tools, so they may be more motivated to engage in learning when they have the opportunity to use a range of equipment. In the case of 'thinking' and 'engaging' behaviours, we may need to be imaginative in thinking of objects that can support them.

**Try this**    **Learning kits**

In addition to the standard classroom equipment that students will hopefully have access to (pens, mini dictionaries, highlighter pens, etc.), encourage them to think of other learning tools they could create and to keep them in a box. For example, they might decide they should have:
- a rectangle of card – for covering text when self-testing
- a reader – a graded book in English to read while waiting for the next task to begin
- a 'new words' box – an empty box to keep new words/flashcards in
- a 'spy hole' – a coin-sized hole in a square of card to use when reading to help focus on specific words (e.g. when looking for errors in a piece of writing)
- a party blower – to interrupt and contribute to a discussion activity
- a dice or home-made spinner – to use in speaking games.

✓ *Getting it right*   **Tools for the job**

For each learning task, ask students to decide which tools they are going to need. To avoid distraction, ask them to put away tools that will not be useful. For homework assignments, include a list of 'required' tools at the top of the sheet.

## Assessing behaviour

One of the reasons why students may be less motivated to engage in learning behaviour is that teachers don't always demand to see it. Consider how activities that may be seen as unpleasant, such as exercise or dieting, are far easier to keep up if we have someone to watch us do them and congratulate us on our efforts. Yet in class we tend to give most attention to assessing outputs of learning, rather than to the processes that lead to them. For example, we frequently set students speaking tasks rather than encourage them to initiate a conversation, or we may design a listening task rather than have them attend to language of their own accord. In doing so, we are signalling to students that simply following instructions is the route to learning and that good learner behaviour has little value. We can strengthen good learner behaviour by designing classroom activities that aim to assess it.

**Try this** ☞ **Learning behaviour presentation**

Ask students to produce a video or presentation about their learning habits at home. They might include a clip from their favourite English TV programme, discuss their favourite English book, or introduce a person they speak to in English. Give positive feedback on the learning behaviours they demonstrate.

**Try this** ☞ **Noticing bingo**

Have students choose a documentary to watch, about a topic they've been studying. Ask them to create a list of five language structures they have studied recently (e.g. comparative adjectives). Students then watch the documentary and tick off the structures when they notice them, writing down the example. The winner is the one who notices the most. Take the lists in and check that they've written the structures accurately.

**Try this** ☞ **Free conversation**

Sit two students opposite each other and give a third a stopwatch. Give the pair two minutes to start and continue a conversation of their choosing. The third student should stop the watch when the pair are unable to keep a 'real' conversation going. Share any particularly successful opening gambits that you overhear.

There are also opportunities to draw attention to learning behaviour during feedback.

✓ *Getting it right* **Feedback**

Focus feedback on the behaviour learners are adopting. If students perform well, praise them for the actions they took, e.g. *All those notes have really expanded your vocabulary!* If they do less well, ask them what they could do to improve the way they learn. If possible, ask them to correct mistakes using the target behaviour, e.g. by looking up a misspelt word in a dictionary.

## Rewards

Reward systems are a familiar way of strengthening positive learner behaviour. Some argue that they can undermine intrinsic motivation, but this depends on how they are perceived. If they are seen as a way of controlling students' behaviour, or as an end in themselves, they might reduce intrinsic motivation. However, these perceptions shouldn't develop if students have a say in organizing the reward system and if they clearly understand the value of the behaviour being rewarded. In addition, rewards can provide reassurance that a learner is going about things in the right way, a gentle reminder if they're not, and evidence that their efforts are being appreciated.

**Try this**  **Token systems**

Use tokens, in the form of points, ink stamps, or gold stars, and add them to a record sheet or chart to reward students. With older learners, allow them to set up the **token system** (also known as *token economies*), deciding what the tokens should look like, what they will be awarded for, at what stage in the lesson the credits will be given out, and even who will award them.

✓ *Getting it right* **Learner-centred rewards**

Give certain students responsibility for awarding credit for positive learning behaviours. Train your helpers to be generous in their interpretation of target behaviour at first, but as time goes on encourage them to be stricter. Let them decide how credit points should be traded in too. For example, they might like to trade points for time spent playing English language computer games at the end of the week.

## Association with reward

As we saw in Chapter 1, pleasurable association is a key aspect of motivation: learners feel well disposed to activities they associate with enjoyment and resentful of doing those they don't. However, although token systems may motivate by offering pleasurable rewards, they don't create a *direct* link between learning behaviour and pleasure. When there is no opportunity to gain rewards, students may give up this behaviour.

Admittedly, many of the learning behaviours identified in this chapter aren't especially enjoyable and may stop learners experiencing pleasure. For example, asking questions creates uncertainty, speaking in English puts communication at risk, and stopping to look up words or take notes delays completion. Even the way we describe some learning activities, such as 'testing yourself', can evoke negative associations.

✓ *Getting it right* **Avoiding trigger words**

Avoid saying words that may trigger negative associations, e.g. *take notes, memorize this list, use a dictionary*. Try to paraphrase with words that have a more positive feel, e.g. *Let's write some ideas down. Can you get it right without looking at your notes? Let's find out what that means.*

It is important, therefore, to make the learning behaviour itself pleasurable so that students will form positive associations with it. The reason for including the party blower and spy hole in the learning kits activity (see page 38) is that they may help students to associate learning behaviours with fun. The principle of linking learning behaviour with positive associations lies behind a recent idea, known as **temptation bundling**, put forward by the behavioural economist Katherine Milkman. This idea suggests that we should do something we like ('temptation') at the same time as doing things we dislike, 'bundling' good and bad. For example, we could watch our favourite TV programme while exerting ourselves on the rowing machine. In this way, we may begin to feel positive towards the 'bundle' as a whole.

**Try this** 👉 **Temptation bundles**

Have students list their favourite activities, e.g. *listening to music, watching TV, eating crisps,* etc. Next to each one, students write down a good learning behaviour that they could engage in at the same time, e.g. *listening to music: reading; watching TV: looking up words; eating crisps: making notes*. Students could also create and share selfies or other photos of themselves doing their temptation bundles. Encourage students to vote on their favourites.

✓ *Getting it right* **Music players**

Consider allowing students to use personal music players when performing learning behaviours independently in class, such as note-taking or revising. Alternatively, play some music on speakers (see Chapter 6 for discussion on background music). This will help create associations with pleasure.

We can also introduce elements of play and competition when learners are engaged in learning behaviours, such as using dictionaries, by adapting popular games to further increase associations with pleasure.

**Try this** 👉 **Running dictionary dictation**

Adapt the popular 'running dictation' activity into one for memorizing words and definitions. Put photocopies of dictionary pages either at the front of the classroom or on a wall outside, and mark several target words and definitions with a highlighter. One student in a pair reads the target words and returns to report them to their partner, who writes them down. The fastest pair to finish writing the words correctly are the winners. The pairs can then swap roles for a second round.

**Try this** 👉 **Simon says**

Agree on a simple instruction and an action for each of the learning habits on page 37. For example: instruction – ask a question; action – raise your hand. Practise by calling out instructions and asking students to do the corresponding actions. Then tell students they must only do the actions if you say 'Simon says' before calling them out. Students who make mistakes must leave the game. Let winners take over the role of calling out instructions.

## Modelling

The point of the game 'Simon says' is that the leader can often trick us into performing an action by doing it themselves. This is because our brains have a **mirroring** system that encourages us to copy the behaviour of other people, whether it's a smile, a gesture, or a dance move.

We can take advantage of this system in a number of ways. Perhaps the simplest is to use photographs or videos. Many learning behaviours (see each of the learning habits on page 37) can be illustrated quite easily. For example, we could illustrate asking a question with a picture of raised hands. By surrounding students with images of good learning behaviours, we increase the likelihood they'll adopt them.

---

**Try this**  **Positive behaviour screen saver**

Ask the class to choose a positive learning behaviour from the 'Learning English Dos and Don'ts' poster (see page 38) and to take a photograph of each other in a pose that illustrates the behaviour. Alternatively, search for a selection of images online for them to choose from. Make a collage of their favourites using one of the many free collage maker websites and use it as a screen saver on the class computer. Make it available to older students so they can use it as a screen saver or background on their own electronic devices.

### ✓ *Getting it right*   Cool photos

Asking students to select their own photos is preferable because they gravitate towards images of young people they think are cool. This is important because the brain's mirroring system works most effectively when we are observing someone we either like or look up to.

Of course, instead of photos we can also use videos. These give students more detail about the target behaviour, and watching someone else get pleasure or improve their self-esteem from doing something can really encourage them to 'have a go'.

---

**Try this**  **Learning models**

Have students search for online video guides to learning behaviours, posted by young people. Topics might include 'how to take notes' or 'my book recommendations'. Alternatively, make some of your students the learning models. Ask a small group to see you after the lesson and invite them to become learning models for the week. For example, suggest that one keeps a reader with them, or takes great class notes. Keep their role a secret and see if their behaviour catches on.

While teachers may not be part of their students' social groups, it is still important that they model target behaviours. Teachers are normally positioned at the front of the class in a very visible position. If they perform the behaviours expected from their students, it can encourage students to mirror them and remind those with limited attention capacity of what they should be doing. If nothing else, it will show that teachers are not asking students to do something they wouldn't want to do themselves.

### ✓ *Getting it right*   Setting an example

Try occasionally to act like a learner yourself. Pretend that some knowledge is new to you and do things you'd expect students to do, such as looking up words or asking questions to yourself. You could also share information about learning behaviour you engage in outside the class, telling students about things you read or lesson vocabulary that you heard being used, for example.

Another advantage of teachers acting as learners themselves (or sharing online video guides to learning behaviours) is that they can show students *how* to perform learning behaviour. Learners have to be able to visualize the steps involved in a task before they can motivate themselves to do it. This is particularly important for habits of thought, such as question formation, which teachers may neglect to demonstrate.

✓ *Getting it right*

### Asking questions

Try to elicit questions about language instead of asking them. For example, write on the board two sentences that reveal the difference between two words or structures and guide students towards a learning question.

The Eiffel tower is a <u>tall</u> building.

Everest is a very <u>high</u> mountain.

These sentences could elicit the learning question: *What's the difference between 'tall' and 'high'?*

It's worth noting that a habit, by definition, is something that demands no motivation at all. If teachers can stimulate good learning behaviour regularly enough in class for it to become a habit, they may reduce the chance of motivation becoming an issue. This is a huge 'if', but shifting the teaching focus from language to behaviour would be a step in this direction.

**Why this works** ⏸️➡️

### Changing behaviour

When we discuss changing behaviour, we often draw on the ideas of **behaviourism**. Early behaviourists thought that the behaviour we engage in is the result of associations with pleasure or displeasure developed from experience. Changing learning behaviour therefore required the teacher to play a dominant role in class, giving out rewards and strict punishments. Many now believe the ideas of behaviourism have limited use in education. Cognitive psychologists argue that we change behaviour by evaluating our activities in response to feedback and deciding whether it helps us achieve our goals. Under this model, the teacher's role is primarily to provide opportunities for assessment and feedback. However, the emphasis behaviourists placed on the quality of experiences and the development of habits should not be overlooked. Rather than simply handing out study skills worksheets from time to time, teachers need to make the procedures for learning central to lessons so that they can be seen as rewarding and familiar. The methods associated with behaviourism may have become outdated, but its emphasis on behaviour hasn't.

# Part 2    The learning context

# 5      Teacher behaviour

Learners strongly associate the subjects they study with the people who teach them. So any pleasure a student feels when they contemplate their studies will depend in part on their view of their teacher. Students who like their teacher may also make efforts to please them by working hard at their subject. A well-liked teacher is therefore a motivating teacher. This means we have to find ways to relate to students and engage them on a personal level.

## Welcoming students

Of course, if a student already has negative feelings towards English, or towards working in an L2, it may be difficult to establish relationships with them while learning activities are taking place. Teachers may sometimes need to take time out from actual teaching to develop rapport.

**Try this**  **Opening conversation**

At the start of the lesson, dedicate five minutes to conversation unrelated to the lesson. Use the students' L1 if necessary. Remain seated to appear as an equal and join conversations students are already having, or introduce topics they are likely to respond to (e.g. a football match, TV programme, or song). Spend time listening and share your opinions and experiences. Establish common ground where possible, but prioritize sincerity and openness. End the conversation with an invitation to join you in learning, such as *Shall we do some learning now?* Regain authority and students' confidence with an assertive *Good afternoon, class. Welcome to your English lesson.*

**✓ Getting it right**    **Late students**

Arriving late may show disrespect, but reacting negatively to late students can damage your attempt at relationship building. Greet students by name enthusiastically as they enter so they don't feel they can slip in unnoticed, and add a 'late mark' to the register. Deal with persistent lateness through the school's discipline procedures.

## Starting work

Making a transition from being relaxed and informal with students to being purposeful and earnest is important. A teacher's commitment to their subject will raise interest and curiosity. After all, if *we* don't take our subject seriously, why should students? But it is essential that we manage this shift without losing rapport.

Many teachers maintain their appeal by injecting enthusiasm or dramatic intensity to proceedings, as a magician might. A fictional character who exemplifies this approach is the English teacher Mr Keating in the film *Dead Poets Society*. He starts his first class by walking calmly to the back of his classroom and out of the door, whistling as he goes, and inviting the boys to join him.

**Try this ☞** | **The unexpected opening**

Start the lesson by taking students out of their comfort zone. For example, invite a volunteer to the front to help you. You could whisper a question to them containing target language and have them write up their answer, before eliciting the question from the class, or start drawing something unexpectedly yourself that will help you present the lesson.

Even target setting can be done in a dramatic, inspiring way. In his 2009 TED talk on leadership, Simon Sinek observes that leaders inspire by first outlining *why* something is being done before saying *how* it will be achieved and *what* this will involve. This approach can be used when we're introducing aims. For example, if you intend to start a lesson on travel by doing an exercise to match phrases and meanings, you might say:

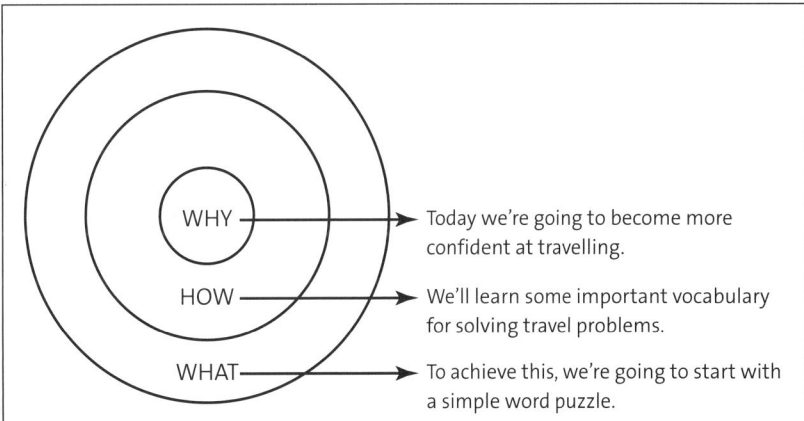

FIGURE 5.1 | *The 'why, how, what' approach to introducing learning aims*

**Try this ☞** | **Exploiting aims**

Once you've produced some carefully worded aims such as those in Figure 5.1, exploit them with a short gap-fill activity. Write the aims on the board, but create gaps for the most emotive words (e.g. *confident, important, solve, simple,* etc.). Write the missing words in a word pool. Have learners complete the aims and then chant the objective together, emphasizing the gapped words.

**✓ *Getting it right*** | **Teacher movement**

Walk around the class as you speak to students and make use of gesture. Controlled movement of the body and hands will keep the focus on you and make you appear relaxed and authoritative. Unexpected pauses and quickened movements will also convey energy and commitment.

# Demotivation

Although it's important to consider how we can *increase* motivation, we must also ensure we don't cause motivation levels to fall. Many students who experience **demotivation** identify their teacher as the reason. We needn't necessarily take this personally – sometimes a student may simply be redirecting personal frustration at an easy target – but when faced with the pressure of getting a group of learners to do something they'd prefer not to do, we sometimes fail to maintain rapport.

One threat to rapport is the perception that we are dominating proceedings, and our attempts to get students engaged may be seen as too forceful. **Student-centred** lesson activities will prevent such perceptions developing, but during teacher-led stages of the lesson we may need to use other strategies.

## Humour

Injecting humour into the classroom can help maintain rapport. Visual humour works particularly well with low-level learners, as it can be understood immediately. Using irony (in the sense of creating unexpected contexts for tasks) when instructing students can help release tension and so make teaching seem less forceful; there are a number of ways we can do this.

**Try this** ☞ **Humorous contexts**

Create a humorous reason for students to do things. The degree to which you pretend or act out the situations will depend on the age of the students and your rapport with them. Here are some examples:
- pretend you've written a letter for the school director and need the students to correct it
- suggest you need their help to spell a difficult word
- before sorting/ordering tasks, pretend to have cards perfectly ordered and then drop them
- pretend you're bored of the classroom wall decoration and student posters are really needed to liven it up
- ask students to set homework for the next lesson and to set some for you too (e.g. marking/research).

Loss of rapport may also happen when students think that the teacher has failed to meet certain needs, such as making them feel valued. Perhaps the most basic of these **esteem needs** is the need for attention. An excuse frequently given by students for not putting effort into a class is: 'The teacher doesn't care about me, so why should I care about her/his lesson?' The effort teachers put into planning and teaching may help students feel more valued to some extent, but it is important to make sure the attention paid to their needs continues during student-centred activities.

## Monitoring

Monitoring of students is not just necessary for giving timely feedback. It also demonstrates that teachers care about students' needs, and can help identify problems with task design (e.g. level of challenge), unclear instructions, or tension between students, before it turns into resentment towards the teacher.

✓ *Getting it right*

**Monitoring**

When monitoring the class, position yourself at the students' eye level. This isn't so easy to do when students are sat at their desks, and crouching or kneeling may be physically uncomfortable for you and psychologically uncomfortable for the students; pulling up a chair for 30 seconds will make the experience much easier. If possible, leave some extra chairs around the classroom before the lesson begins to help you. (Note that this will also help you move students between groups.) Show you were listening by feeding back to the whole class on any interesting chats you've had with individual students.

Nevertheless, it is not enough simply to give students attention. They are acutely aware of lack of fairness, and teachers must ensure that both attention and support are distributed evenly among them.

**Try this** ☞ **Video observation**

When you are next observed teaching a class, ask your observer to video you. Watch the video and count the number of times you look and smile at each side of the classroom, and the amount of time you spend in each part of the class. Then compare the results with the seating plan and identify any unevenness in your attention. You may find that louder or less well-behaved students are being given a greater share of attention, whereas students who seem passive and unengaged are receiving less.

## Control

Perhaps the biggest threat to student motivation is a feeling on their part that they are being judged unfavourably and unfairly. Sometimes the pressure *we* feel to reach teaching objectives can make us a little impatient when we correct or discipline students. However, students will rarely see their own behaviour as inappropriate and are likely to conclude that the teacher doesn't understand them, or even dislikes them.

✓ *Getting it right*

**Discipline**

Try to appear calm and neutral when student behaviour doesn't meet expectations. Write up agreed lesson targets on the board so that your expectations remain clear. Then, when you want to let students know that you need their attention, use a signal they have agreed with you (e.g. placing your bag on the desk). Thank them for their cooperation.

A sense of unfairness may also develop if students feel their efforts have not been recognized. Teachers must be sure to take students' efforts seriously, even if they do not appear to have made much effort. It is also likely that the quality of their contributions will increase if they believe they are going to be taken seriously.

**Try this** ☞ **Named sentences**

On the board, write sentences that students contribute to an activity and, as you do so, add the student's first name beside each one. The contribution could include an opinion suggested during a discussion or a sentence you've elicited. Correct any minor errors as you write, then check the student is happy with the sentence and thank them. Thereafter, refer to the sentence using the student's name:

> The reason I like Nawar's sentence is that she's used a great adjective ...
> Could we make Ablai's sentence even better?
> Don't forget Michele's clever idea about the crowds of tourists ...

## Pacing

Motivation may also be at risk when students feel time is not being used appropriately. Many will look for praise when they finish tasks quickly, and may be resentful if they are made to wait for slower students. At the same time, slower students may resent not being allowed enough time to complete tasks.

**Try this**  **Countdown timers**

Agree with students the time needed to complete tasks before each learning activity begins. Set the time on a countdown timer (available online and on most interactive whiteboards) and make sure students can see it. Give more of your assistance to students who appear to be struggling to complete the task in the time allowed. Agree on time extensions with the whole class.

✓ *Getting it right*   **Fast-finisher activities**

Be sure to have a range of extension tasks in mind to serve as fast-finisher activities, but avoid giving fast finishers extra materials as this will make slower students feel they are missing out. Letting some start homework early will also make slower students feel disadvantaged. Fast-finisher activities should bring benefits to all class members. For example, they may involve helping other students, or finding out the meaning of a key word from the lesson and writing the definition on the board.

## Feedback

Self-esteem is particularly at risk during feedback, when struggling, lower-level students may feel they are being compared unfavourably to others, or that their efforts aren't being valued. The risk that students will jump to such conclusions is greatest when the teacher provides written comments, which can't be delivered with an encouraging tone of voice.

✓ *Getting it right*   **Written feedback**

Record grades in mark books, but avoid adding a grade to every piece of work you return to students. This will help them focus on learning rather than performance standards, and avoid demotivating comparisons being made. You can always tell students their grades individually at a later point. Avoid making negative comments on their homework; simply state what you liked about it and what could be done better next time. For example:

*I loved all your adjectives and adverbs – now let's make spelling a priority ...*
*I really enjoyed reading these ideas – now think about using paragraphs to structure them.*

If feedback can be given orally, this will make it more encouraging since we can give positive non-verbal signals, such as smiling.

**Try this** ☞ **Video feedback**

If your students submit work electronically, record one minute's video feedback for each of them, using screencasting software such as Jing. Screencasting allows you to record what is visible on your screen, along with your spoken commentary. You will receive a link to each recording which you can share with students, for example by copying and pasting to the class's Learning Management System.

Although feedback can sometimes put motivation at risk, it also provides an opportunity to show that the teacher cares; and assuming we have managed to create and maintain rapport through our feedback, the thought of our reaction and the desire to please us may even drive students to try harder. For this reason, reacting openly to any of our students' efforts, either with pleasure or even (uncritical) disappointment, is always a good idea.

✓ *Getting it right*

**Incorrect answers**

Show hope and expectation when a student offers an answer in class, as if they were a member of your favourite sports team trying to score. Let out an enthusiastic *Yes!* or *Great!* for valid answers, or a comment to show that you value the attempt:

*Good try – I can see exactly why you thought that.*
*Oh, so close! You're almost there!*

# Ending lessons

At the end of the lesson, teachers can strengthen the students' sense of obligation towards them by making them aware of the care that has been put into the preparation of their lesson. We can do this subtly by asking students what they thought of the class. This may also provide an outlet for any ill feeling before it threatens motivation.

**Try this** ☞ **Feedback slips**

At the end of each week, give out slips of paper asking for feedback like the example below. The fewer the questions, the happier students will be to respond. Collect the papers, but don't insist that students put their names on them.

| How much do you agree? Circle the face that matches your opinion. | | | |
|---|:---:|:---:|:---:|
| This week … | | | |
| The teacher tried to make the lessons interesting. | ☺ | ☺ | ☹ |
| The teacher gave me an opportunity to practise. | ☺ | ☺ | ☹ |
| I received help from the teacher when I needed it. | ☺ | ☺ | ☹ |
| I feel the teacher valued the contributions I made. | ☺ | ☺ | ☹ |
| I know what I have to do for homework and I can do it. | ☺ | ☺ | ☹ |
| Any sad faces? Tell me why! | | | |

FIGURE 5.2   *Feedback slips*

**Try this** ☞   **Lesson previews**

You can also make the task of motivating students easier by sharing some information about the next lesson (e.g. *On Monday we'll learn some phrases that will really help you make new friends.*) to help increase their expectations. Setting preparatory homework (e.g. to watch a video on a related topic) will also raise their curiosity.

✓ *Getting it right*   **Thanking students**

It's worth remembering too that students have (hopefully) been doing what we wanted them to do for an hour or so. Thank students as they leave the classroom and comment on any positive contributions they made. This will help them feel appreciated.

**Why this works** ⫸   **Relating to students**

From the 1990s onwards, researchers started seeing motivation as something that depends on the relationships formed in the learning context, particularly between student and teacher. Dörnyei's 1994 three-level framework of L2 motivation, for example, identifies the teacher as a central factor in motivation (see *Useful websites*). More recently, a group of researchers led by Gregory Montalvo found that students who liked their teachers were more disciplined and focused when they did their assignments. Among the reasons participants gave for trying hard were a desire to be accepted by their teacher and to show respect for them.

# 6     The learning environment

In the 1940s, the educator Loris Malaguzzi claimed there were three teachers in every classroom. There is the teacher, of course. Then there are the students, who learn from each other. And finally, there is the learning environment itself. Malaguzzi's point was that classrooms, just like teachers, can draw students to them and encourage learning.

## Using space

Experts argue that on entering the class students should gain a sense that they are free to move and come together. Well-spaced tables, or 'horseshoe' arrangements, in which students can face each other, will help promote collaborative learning and interaction. Of course, we may not have a say in classroom furniture arrangements, or want students to talk in every class, but where possible we should use furniture to ensure students are motivated to interact in the way we intend them to.

 *Getting it right*

### Furniture

If you have a say in choosing classroom furniture, suggest providing students with chairs on castors (small wheels) to allow groups to be formed flexibly, and recommend small, lightweight, movable desks. Ensure unused furniture is stacked away and that students have easy access to both a central activity space and the main board. This will allow them to participate fully in the lesson.

Although we may all have a favourite classroom arrangement that we believe works effectively, it's a good idea to be open to change. We all love to enter and explore new spaces, and unchanging rooms that we have little control over can rapidly reduce our levels of **stimulation**.

**Try this** ☞ **Self-organization**

Outline planned activities to students at the beginning of the class. Then, on the board, draw squares representing desks and ask students to suggest an appropriate arrangement of the furniture. Be prepared to intervene if you feel their idea won't work for your plans. Once a plan is agreed, ask students to move the furniture into place themselves. This will give them a sense of control over their environment and create a willingness to try out the arrangement they have created.

**Try this** ☞ **Creating new spaces**

Students will find spaces that they can retreat to appealing. Reading 'dens', and even 'class cinema' areas, are often used by teachers to create attractive zones that can inspire different moods. If they are available in your school, use free-standing partition screens to help you organize space in motivating ways.

**Try this** ☞ **Leaving the classroom**

Take students out of the classroom and the school building as much as possible. Use the space outside to have them do 'running dictations' (i.e. fix a text on a wall and have one member of each pair go back and forth reporting it to the other, who sits at a distance with a notebook). Set up conversations at a distance, or drills in which they throw a ball between them in a circle as they say months, days of the week, and so on.

# The social environment

Students need an environment that encourages the development of self-esteem, fairness, and inclusion. For younger learners this can involve creating a sense of belonging and security. As students grow older, developing identity and gaining acceptance from their peers become more important. This is particularly the case in a language classroom, as use of an L2 can exclude students who are less able to use it, and prevent them from expressing their identity.

A great way of building self-esteem is to display photos students have taken, or to use them as a resource, since this allows us to acknowledge their creativity and to celebrate them and their lives. The importance of fairness and inclusion can be underlined by posters.

**Try this** ☞ **Selfie display**

Bring a camera into class. Think of a sentence that students could complete to reveal something about themselves, such as *I'm crazy about* … or *I want to be a* … . Have each student write a word to complete the sentence on a large piece of paper (or a small board) and take a selfie. Print the selfies and create a wall display, using the sentence opening as a header. You could link the sentence to current language you're studying.

**Try this** ☞ **Respect poster**

Negotiate a set of class rules with the students in their L1. Make sure they generate the ideas, but guide them. One interesting way of doing this is to suggest that every rule starts with the word *Respect*:
• Respect the teacher.
• Respect others.
• Respect the class environment.
• Respect your future self.
Write ideas on the board and discuss how to apply the rules in an English-language lesson, e.g. being patient while listening to others speak.

**Try this** ☞ **Celebrities**

Start the lesson by making someone a celebrity. Say they've become famous because of their excellent homework or their English skills. Invite them to come and sit in the 'celebrity chair' (the teacher's chair) while peers applaud, and then interview them as a 'celebrity'. Be sure to remind students of the 'respect' rules on page 54 before you begin. 'A or B' preference questions work well for interviews, e.g. *Which do you think is more important – love or money?* Encourage the 'celebrity' to take a selfie with their adoring fans (their peers) behind them.

## Grouping students

When it comes to grouping students, teachers face a dilemma. Friends may be happier if they can sit near each other, and may even resent a teacher who tries to separate them. What's more, students may not enjoy coming to class if they are made to sit with someone they feel uncomfortable working with. However, friends often distract each other in class if their priorities are to bond socially, and their behaviour can be seen as cliquey and resented by other students.

✓ *Getting it right*   **Friendship groups**

In classes where motivation is an issue, avoid allowing friends to sit with each other. However, do ask students in private if there are any peers they dislike working with.

Moreover, classwork is likely to be more productive if we ensure that those who are most motivated to engage in activities work with those who are less engaged. For shorter tasks we might compromise by giving students some choice over who they work with (see the 'Grouping by response' activity below). For longer activities, we may feel it necessary to determine groups before class starts and then strengthen commitment to groups during the activities (see the 'Group names' activity below).

**Try this** ☞ **Grouping by response**

We can often see who is most motivated when we invite students to stand. Give those students who stand up first the instructions for the task you've planned and invite them to find two or three other students to perform the task with.

**Try this** ☞ **Group names**

Establish groups at the beginning of the week and invite each group to give themselves a team name. They could base the names on the learning topic; for example, in a week when the topic is transport, they could choose 'rockets', 'submarines', 'double-deckers', etc. Encourage a spirit of cooperation by referring to the team names during group activities, e.g. *The double-deckers are writing beautifully.*

## Wall space and decoration

Teachers who are lucky enough to have all their lessons in the same room often go to great lengths to decorate the learning space. They cover walls, doors, drawer fronts, and desks with warm, bright colours and imaginative displays, and they use boxes, trays, and holders to create neat, ordered spaces. Attractive environments like these create a positive mood and increase learners' willingness to engage.

## Learning dispositions

Wall displays are sometimes used to promote specific learning attitudes. We might, for example, want to focus on the 'seven thinking dispositions' identified by Harvard University – adventure, caution, clarity, curiosity, evaluation, planning, and self-awareness – or some of the learning behaviours discussed in Chapter 4, such as reading for pleasure.

A particularly important function of the language classroom is to raise curiosity towards target cultures by including maps, film posters, etc. The priorities set will depend on a number of factors, such as education policies, your culture, and the age and gender of your students.

---

**Try this**  **Wall audit**

List the learning dispositions which are priorities for your class. Consult with department heads, colleagues, and students. You could use a survey like the one below to see if students agree with your list.

This classroom encourages me to:
- ask questions to the teacher or my friends
- make mistakes without feeling embarrassed
- look for new ways to do things
- take pride and care in my work.

Search the internet to see how other teachers encourage their target dispositions through displays. You might, for instance, find a poster entitled 'Asking questions' with question openers such as *How do you say* ... ? Show students examples you've found and dedicate a lesson to reproducing ones they like.

There are plenty of different ways to turn statements about dispositions into poster-friendly texts. Examples include slogans (*today's reader, tomorrow's leader*) or lists (*ten ways to give examples*). Figure 6.1 shows an example of an acrostic and a meme.

✓ *Getting it right*   **Choosing decorations**

Allow students to participate as much as possible in choosing decorations for the classroom, or in creating their own materials for display. This will increase not only their sense of control over their environment but also their understanding of the messages you're trying to communicate through the decorations.

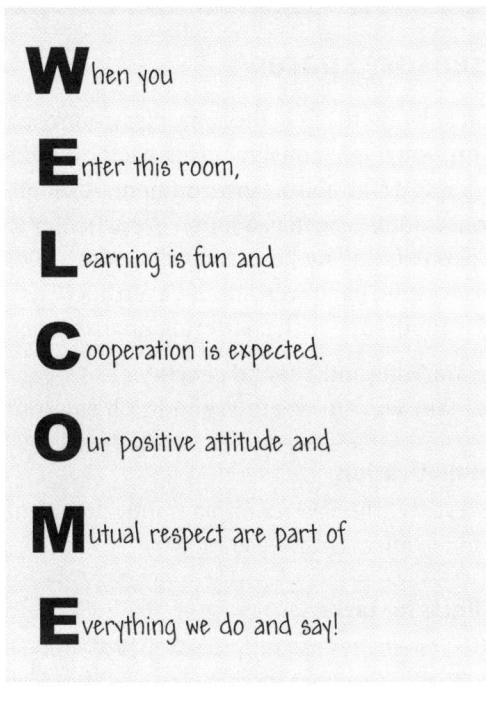

FIGURE 6.1    *Classroom posters for learning dispositions*

**Try this**     **Write your own acrostic**

Give your students an example of an acrostic about learning dispositions (e.g. *ACE: Adventurous, Curious, Engaged*). Then give them a short word and, in groups, ask them to write their own acrostic. To make the task less challenging, give them the first few words of each line. You could also give one suggestion in brackets. Here is an example of an acrostic with *SHINE*:

Sit _____ (still)
Help your _____ (peers)
Insist on _____ (neat work)
Never _____ (give up)
Enjoy _____ (study)

We can create positive moods and messages through the visual decoration we use. For instance, an 'enchanted forest' or 'castle' decoration/poster at the doorway of your classroom could represent the idea of using language adventurously. Such decorations are particularly popular with younger learners, but posters can work well with all ages.

**✓ Getting it right**    **Digital displays**

If you are unable to leave work on walls permanently, create digital copies of temporary displays by photographing them and adding them to a PowerPoint file. Playing the files in a slideshow loop from time to time may in fact interest students more than having their work on constant display.

## Multisensory spaces

If you don't always teach in the same classroom or are unable to use decoration, you might consider using background music, sound, or even smell to create a stimulating environment. After all, the real world engages all our senses, and we can use sound in particular to transport students into realistic contexts and make lessons seem more relevant. Some sound effects, such as a crowded bar or restaurant, even allow us to create an English-language soundscape with chattering English voices.

Access to YouTube and a sound effects website, e.g. www.soundsnap.com, provides many ways to create a sound-rich environment.

**Try this** ☞ **Music for motivation**

As students enter the classroom, play motivational music (e.g. the *Rocky* theme tune) or sound effects (e.g. cheering).

**Try this** ☞ **Sound effects for tasks**

Sound effects websites usually provide lists of sound effects for specific contexts. Choose a context for speaking tasks from your preferred website, for example a zoo or an airport arrivals lounge. Have volunteers click on appropriate sound effects as other students speak and encourage speakers to improvise reactions. For example, on hearing a roar they might say, 'Look, a lion!'

**Try this** ☞ **Mood music**

For reading tasks, choose music that enhances the mood: Philip Glass's 'Façades' is ideal for a scary story, and jungle sound effects may enhance a text about rainforests.

✓ *Getting it right* **Background music**

When using background music, choose pieces with few changes in tempo, volume, or pitch. Easy listening or piano music will tend not to distract. Be mindful of cultural sensitivities, especially with respect to Western music and videos, and be aware that some students may find the sound of any music distracting.

**Try this** ☞ **Scent survey**

Tell students they are going to choose a smell for the classroom that week. Put a drop of an essential oil (e.g. lemon, lavender, or peppermint) on three separate slips of card and pass them around. Ask students to give scores out of ten for each, depending on the extent to which it makes them feel a) happy, b) relaxed, and c) awake. Appoint a 'scent monitor' and ask them to put a drop of the chosen scent on cotton wool in each corner of the classroom every day.

It is important for people to touch things around them, using what is known as their 'haptic' sense. This is especially true of young people, and denying them this opportunity can cause frustration. Yet language classrooms usually offer few occasions to use our sense of touch, and we should find opportunities to engage students practically in lessons.

**Try this** ☞ **Paper and realia**

Look for times when students can cut, tear, and pile paper, for example during communication or vocabulary games. During classwork, allow students to scrunch up used pieces of paper and throw them in the bin. Additionally, give students opportunities to use objects from their bags as props or prompts.

**Try this** ☞ **Cuisenaire rods**

Cuisenaire rods (coloured sticks of varying length) are fun for learners of all ages. Each colour or length can be used to represent features of language, such as parts of speech, primary and secondary stress, or even the nouns in a story. Students can listen to sentences and then order rods to show they've understood a sequence of events, stress pattern, or sentence structure, or pick up rods when they hear a corresponding word. Alternatively, they can use them as building blocks and practise explaining what their creations represent.

**Try this** ☞ **Foldables and sticky notes**

Flat posters can be made far more engaging by adding tactile components, such as 'foldables' - pieces of paper that can be lifted up to reveal text or an image underneath. Search for design ideas online. Older learners may enjoy using sticky notes. Invite them to have conversations in writing by posting up starter questions for each other and creating a 'thread' of responses (see the 'Virtual chatrooms' activity on page 83).

**Why this works** ▏▎▶

> **Opening up spaces**
>
> Young people spend a significant amount of time in the classroom. Indeed, children of primary school age may spend more waking hours in their school classroom than in any other space. Our environment influences our moods and level of stimulation, which can influence relationships and learning potential. Experts argue that, all too often, plain classroom walls and furniture enclose and trap students physically and mentally, demanding that they submit to the teacher and leave the real world behind. We need to open up learning spaces to students and open up the classroom to the outside world. In doing so, we can make sure our school environments are not simply adequate but sources of inspiration.

# 7　Learner roles: independence and responsibility

Though we depend on others for a feeling of acceptance and self-esteem, we also need to feel a sense of independence. Indeed, this is often considered a basic human need, and we will be drawn to activities that we can control and which we can carry out at a time and place of our choosing. In theory, the same applies to learning tasks. If learners are able to succeed while they have a significant degree of control, they should feel a sense of mastery, which will sustain their motivation.

However, giving learners complete independence is not always appropriate or straightforward. Inexperienced learners do not necessarily know how to learn effectively, and may not have developed the habits and self-confidence necessary to tackle learning independently. These skills and habits must be taught and nurtured if they are to flourish. Furthermore, handing over complete control of the learning process is clearly impractical in typical teaching contexts. Many responsibilities will inevitably remain the teacher's – particularly in terms of ensuring syllabus objectives are met or maintaining discipline – and we may feel our ability to fulfil these obligations is compromised if we give learners too much independence. There may also be some barriers to promoting independence, including a lack of willingness on the part of the students.

Establishing a suitable line between exercising authority and granting freedom is no simple task. This chapter will explore the pressures that often prevent us giving up control, and the steps we can realistically take to help our students to become independent learners.

## Barriers to achieving independence

Students may resist becoming independent learners for several reasons. First among them is fear. The psychological impact of failing can be greater when we have worked independently. This is because, while students who simply follow instructions can always blame failings on the teacher, those who study by themselves will feel more responsible for failings.

It is therefore important to try and create a learning climate that minimizes fear of negative assessment, particularly before testing. Students need to know that, while we are encouraging them to take responsibility for their *learning,* we are not handing them responsibility for their *results*.

✓ *Getting it right*

**Assessment**

Discuss weak performances positively with students and emphasize collective responsibility. After tests, use the pronoun *we* to refer to performance, e.g. *We didn't get many points for this task*. Discuss with students how time in and out of class could be used more effectively to help them in their preparation, and move quickly on to an action plan for future learning.

We can extend this approach to error correction, making sure our language remains positive.

✓ *Getting it right*

**Corrections**

When giving corrective feedback, use the expression *learning opportunity* in place of *mistake* or *error*. For example, write up students' mistakes under the heading *Learning opportunities*. Use the verb *improve* instead of *correct*, e.g. *How can we improve this sentence?*

A student's background (see Chapter 11) may also influence their attitude to independence. The presence of strong authority figures in some students' lives can lead to **learned helplessness**, or a tendency to submit to control. Other students may still be struggling to gain a sense of independence from adults, and may see a teacher's attempt to give them **autonomy** as an excuse to challenge authority. Recent experiences of teacher control can sometimes contribute to these problems, reinforcing learned helplessness and the idea that the teacher is only there to 'force' students into learning. In both cases, a sudden removal of classroom restrictions can be met with incomprehension, and students may find it difficult to adjust.

✓ *Getting it right*

**Explaining reasons**

When you experiment with allowing students to control aspects of the learning process, make sure you carefully explain the reasons why you're doing it. This will allow you to maintain respect and authority while handing over control.

Expectations placed on teachers may also undermine our intention to promote independence. In particular, the pressure to prepare students to perform in exams may lead teachers to look for shortcuts to help cover the syllabus more quickly. It's far quicker to give students information than have them research it.

**Try this** ☞ **Self-study**

Set aside simpler sections of your syllabus for self-study. At the start of term, provide students with a version of the exam syllabuses in simple terms they will understand, marking where you'd like them to direct their own learning. Arrange for students to have self-study sessions periodically, preferably with access to internet resources.

So many classroom tasks are considered the teacher's responsibility (setting deadlines, organizing classrooms, etc.) that we may expose ourselves to criticism if we don't perform them. In addition, we may actually enjoy sharing our knowledge directly, instead of allowing students to discover it for themselves, but the potential pleasure to be gained from teaching empowered, independent learners should compensate for this.

# Developing independence

## Discovery learning

Consider for a moment the difference between learning and discovering. When we learn, we gain knowledge about something that others, for example teachers, already know about. They ask the questions and we attempt to answer them. When we discover, we ask the questions for ourselves. Therefore, if we can make learning more like a process of discovery, by training students to ask questions, we will give them a feeling of independence.

**Try this** ☞ **Lesson questions**

In place of using questions provided in coursebooks, have students write their own. In reading and listening lessons, give students topics and ask them to write what they'd like to know and, for speaking lessons, ask students to write questions for discussion. In grammar lessons, elicit questions about structures. Write the topic on the board, e.g. *Present perfect vs past simple*, and have students brainstorm questions (in their L1 if necessary) such as *Which tense is more common?* At the end of the lesson, decide which questions have been answered; the rest can be explored for homework. (See also 'Asking questions' on page 43.)

We can extend the discovery approach to methods of learning too. Teaching study skills (such as note-taking, using a dictionary, or vocabulary learning) already promotes independence, but we risk undermining this when we advise students on the best ways to learn. Having students share ideas and discuss approaches will give them a sense of freedom and the confidence to find their own strategies.

**Try this** ☞ **Study choices**

Randomly select ten nouns and ten adjectives (at the students' level). On the board, write five of the words in red, five in blue, five in green, and five in yellow, assigning colours randomly. Tell students that they have one minute to try to memorize all 20 words. Now cover the board and ask students to recall as many words as they can. Students then discuss in groups how they tried to remember them (e.g. did they remember words in colour groups, or try to connect words of similar meaning?). Students then share ideas and compare which worked best.

## Peer-teaching

We may even try to involve learners directly in teaching and assessment. Aside from giving a greater sense of independence, this will improve levels of feedback and interaction, which in turn will build mutual trust and cooperation.

**Try this** ☞ **Giving learners the answer keys**

After grammar or vocabulary exercises, put students into A/B pairs. Get Student As to face the board, and Student Bs to face their partner. Put the answer key on the board and have Student As elicit the correct answer from their partner, without saying the answers themselves.

**Try this** ☞ **Self- and peer-assessment**

Encourage self- and peer-assessment of essays by setting very clear assessment criteria that students can understand and apply. For example, you could tell them to score one point for every adjective used, or for every attempt to use the past continuous. Ask them to grade their own work, or that of their peers, before handing it in to you for checking.

Peer-teaching of grammar can be made possible by focusing on grammar words or chunks, rather than structures (for example, *since* rather than *the present perfect*), as these are easier for learners to identify and discuss by themselves. With enough examples, they may then be able to work out rules independently.

**Try this** ☞ **Examples I found**

Ask students to run an internet search for sentences containing target grammar, e.g. *if I were* or *in two days*. Then write up the examples they find. Check the meaning of each sentence is clear by discussing who said it and why. Then encourage them to complete their own rule, e.g. *We use 'if I were' when we want to …* , before discussing their ideas.

✔ *Getting it right* **Search terms**

Students may need guidance to help them return high-quality search results. Familiarize them with useful search operators (keyboard characters that help modify searches). For example, the following search will instruct a search engine to find sentences on BBC websites that begin 'I haven't' and include 'for' or 'since': *site:bbc.co.uk "I haven't * since OR for"*.

In vocabulary classes, students may be given even more scope for peer-teaching, since word meanings can often be communicated more easily than grammar knowledge.

**Try this** ☞ **Vocabulary Venns**

Get students to draw Venn diagrams showing how lexical concepts overlap (see Figure 7.1). Provide each group of students with a different Venn diagram to complete. The circles should represent three closely related L2 nouns (e.g. *train*, *coach*, *bus*). Groups then discuss ways in which the concepts are similar or different, writing their ideas into the corresponding segments (in their L1 if necessary). Alternatively, you could provide three descriptive categories in which students can write a set of target words. For example, they might put animals into the categories *walk*, *swim*, and *fly*. Prepare a series of questions for the students, e.g. *How is a bus similar to a coach?* Invite groups to find the answers from each other's posters.

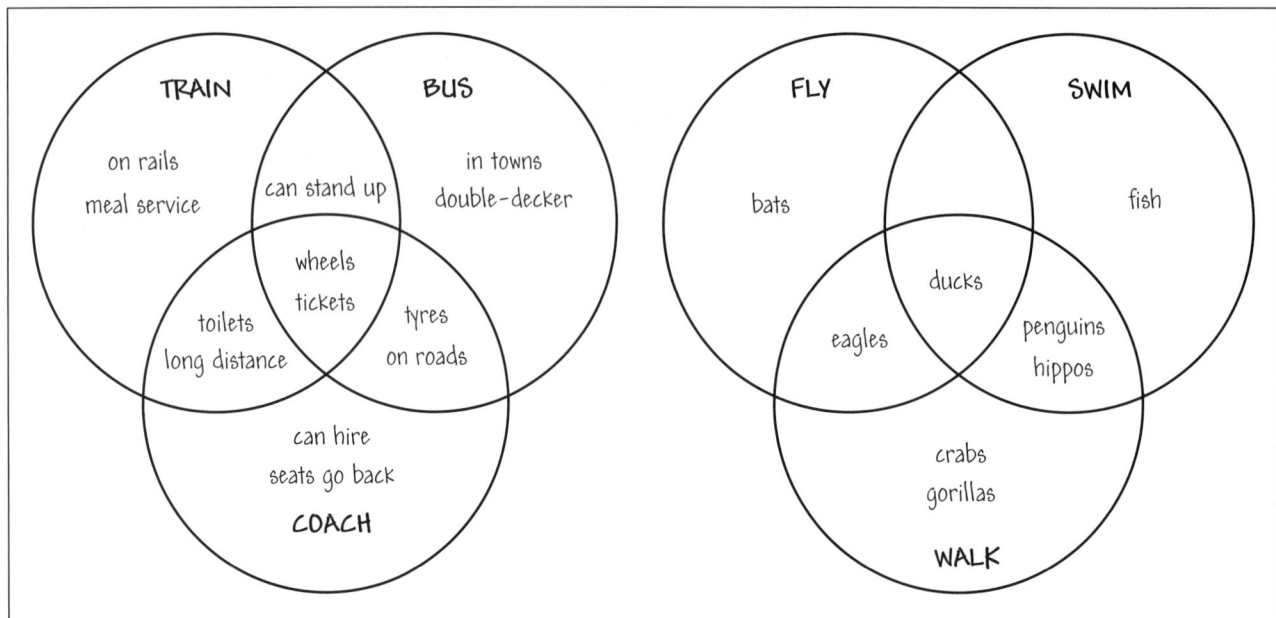

FIGURE 7.1    *Vocabulary Venn diagrams for transport and animal vocabulary*

 **Getting it right**

### Asking peers

Establish peer-support routines in your class, such as *Ask three other students before you ask the teacher*. Ask students if they feel confident about certain topics and identify those who do to the class so that weaker students know who to ask for support.

## Roles and responsibilities

We could also try giving students responsibility for other classroom tasks that are usually the teacher's responsibility. This might include assisting with lesson preparation, preparing discussion material for skills lessons, and even taking on classroom management roles. We could, for instance, put particular students in charge of certain classroom resources, e.g. dictionaries. Such steps will help challenge students' assumptions about responsibility for learning.

**Try this** ☞ **Photo-sourcing**

Whenever you plan to start a lesson with photos, ask students to find examples on their smartphones (if they are permitted), or to find pictures from magazines at home. For example, when doing lessons on describing appearance, have them select images of people to describe. This will show students that they are not dependent on the teacher for finding prompts that will help them produce language.

**Try this** ☞ **Setting homework**

When setting homework, ask students to decide what they need to do to practise the teaching point. For example, if they've been studying comparatives, ask them what items they could compare for homework. Write up the homework on the board, and then ask students to copy them down (or take a photograph if allowed). Agree on a time limit and/or a deadline.

**✓ *Getting it right***

## Classroom resources

Give students as much access as possible to the class board(s) and resources. During class work, invite volunteers to come and write up ideas rather than feed back to you from their seats. Encourage students to share English resources they have found, like songs or websites, on a notice board, and label drawers so students know where to find things.

**Try this** ☞

## Sharing expertise

Ask students to prepare a short presentation on something they know a lot about. They could demonstrate something, hold a question-and-answer session about their hobby, or prepare some photos to share with the class.

**Try this** ☞

## Student roles

Think of classroom roles your students would enjoy. Create names and badges for each role and assign them at the beginning of each week, for example:

**Word watcher:** spot unknown words that appear in texts during the lesson and write them up neatly on a board or on slips of paper, depending on the class's system for reviewing vocabulary.

**Meanings master:** look up definitions of words, as required. Allow students to check your spellings too by making mistakes deliberately.

**Collocation kings:** use a collocations dictionary to check for possible collocations, or a search engine to see which collocations are more common online, e.g. *gain a medal* vs *win a medal*. Students can search for both at the same time (with each enclosed in speech marks) and see how many results are returned.

**✓ *Getting it right***

## Control of mobile devices

Banning mobile devices may undermine the students' sense of independence. If allowing mobile devices in the classroom is not practical, however, consider creating roles that allow certain students to use them provided they keep them visible and on their desks. You might, for example, allow someone to check spelling (using a speech-to-text function), find photos to illustrate new vocabulary, or even make a video of the lesson so that students can review it later on.

**Why this works**

## Learner independence

Since the 1950s, psychologists have recognized that control (or **locus of control**) is one of the pillars of intrinsic motivation, and educationalists have long since discussed ways in which we can make the classroom more learner-centred. Interest in the idea of giving students control has grown recently thanks to research done by Sugata Mitra (see *Useful websites*), who noted the enthusiasm with which young people will gather around computer screens to research and learn independently. Few would suggest that the role of the language teacher can be replaced. Studying words, texts, skills, and grammar requires graded exposure, regular repetition and reviewing, and interaction with language speakers. Nevertheless, it is important to note that, when left to develop their own methods of learning in social groups, students can come alive with enthusiasm.

# 8    Motivating materials

Nowadays, teachers are spoiled for choice when it comes to lesson materials. Coursebooks still provide the backbone for many language courses, but they are now just one of many possible resources. In particular, many teachers will exploit authentic materials online, which have made it far easier to tailor content to individual interests. As regards motivation, the assumption is often that authentic texts are more stimulating, provided we are able to 'grade' them appropriately for the level of our students. However, the secret is more likely to lie in the careful and varied use of materials.

## Coursebooks

Coursebooks are particularly important in English classes. Few other subjects demand such careful graded exposure to material, or such regular reviewing and testing. And of course they are often part of a package of materials that includes support websites and teacher resource packs. But although coursebooks offer learners valuable support, they can also put motivation at risk. Table 8.1 shows how they can both strengthen and weaken motivation.

| Sources of motivation | Sources of demotivation |
| --- | --- |
| Turning the pages, recycling, and testing give students a sense of progress. | Topics and references date quickly and so seem unconnected to the student's world. |
| Grading of language allows students to feel they've mastered texts. | Repetitive style and format of lessons can reduce expectation of pleasure/interest. |
| Carefully staged lessons make lesson aims feel achievable. | Unnatural language, e.g. scripted dialogues, makes tasks seem less useful for the real world. |
| Connected resources make choice and novelty possible. | Non-authentic material doesn't provide opportunities for integration with a community of English language users. |
| Ownership of a coursebook (that students can explore) puts students in control of learning. | Failing to finish the coursebook can cause frustration. |

TABLE 8.1    *Sources of motivation and demotivation in coursebooks*

Whether the advantages of a coursebook will outweigh the disadvantages depends largely on the quality of the material. A well-written coursebook can be a great source of motivation despite any potential disadvantages, just as poor authentic resources or online materials will demotivate. Much will therefore depend on the choice of coursebook.

✓ *Getting it right*    **Choosing coursebooks**

If you are able to choose between coursebooks, consider their likely impact on motivation by asking whether they:
- include puzzles/problems that students can solve
- include self-help opportunities to promote learning independence
- contain stories and objectives that build from unit to unit
- have topics and tasks that draw on existing interests/priorities
- have a coherent group of unit goals that stretch but don't overwhelm students
- feature lively design, humour, and information that adds to existing knowledge
- let students answer questions with existing knowledge and produce language about themselves.

Students' reactions to the coursebook will also depend on their own experiences. One major issue is overcoming their sense that they have 'done this before'. Students may well have explored certain language structures in private language schools, previous schools, or even independently. Confronting a particular lesson topic for a second time may be a good learning strategy, but it will do little to increase motivation. This issue will be particularly relevant where students vary in their proficiency levels, and the coursebook will be more widely accepted if we acknowledge this issue.

✓ *Getting it right*    **Presenting a coursebook**

Acknowledge to students that they will already know some of the topics in their coursebook. Explain that you're going to use their existing knowledge to help them revise where necessary and to give them practice in using English more effectively.

**Try this** ☞    **Testing before teaching**

Give students a grammar exercise from the accompanying workbook or unit test *before* they start the coursebook lesson/unit. Students discuss the answers in groups and write them on a separate sheet of paper (one for each group). As groups finish, collect their sheets. Write the number of correct answers at the bottom of each sheet and ask each group to calculate their percentage score. Then write the following on the board:

1   90%     I understand this topic well. My target is to use the language more fluently.

2   50–90%   I understand a lot of this, but revision will be useful.

3   <50%     This topic is important, and I need to understand it better.

Groups then identify which category they belong to. Record the results on the board and summarize what they reveal about the students' current understanding and their learning needs.

## Exploiting course materials

The degree to which the coursebook will motivate learners will also depend on the teacher's skill in exploiting it, and there are several traps to avoid.

First, the printed page reveals material to students all at once, so there is less room left for arousing curiosity. Compare that to the dramatic beginning of a film, which reveals music, title, setting, and characters in sequence.

**Try this** ☞ **The slow reveal**

Reveal features of a lesson or a text one at a time. If you have the digital version of a coursebook, you could zoom in on a title or a photo, for example. Otherwise, write up titles on the board, or find photos of places/people mentioned in the text. Encourage students to predict lesson themes based on the titles or photos and discuss existing experiences of the topic. Then write key words from the lesson on the board and ask students to guess their significance.

✓ *Getting it right*　**Books closed start**

Establish a need for the coursebook before using it in class. For example, after introducing a lesson topic, you might say *There's some good information on this in the coursebook – shall we have a look?* or *There are some good examples of this tense in the coursebook.*

Second, using a coursebook inevitably involves spending time looking down. This means there may be less opportunity for rewarding social interaction. As the lesson progresses, it's important to find frequent opportunities for students to close their coursebooks and work together. There are many ways to do this.

**Try this** ☞ **Photograph the exercise**

Have students photograph exercises (e.g. a vocabulary gap fill) with a mobile device (if allowed), and then close their coursebooks. Students are now free to walk around the classroom and carry out the task orally with other students. They then return to their coursebooks and write down the answers.

**Try this** ☞ **Transfer to whiteboard**

Copy simple exercises, such as putting words in categories, onto a whiteboard. Do this before the lesson or, alternatively, have students call words out: give them a challenge by asking for the words in alphabetical order, or make deliberate spelling mistakes for them to correct.

**Try this** ☞ **Close and remember**

After doing an exercise, ask students to close their coursebooks and see how many of the sentences or words they can remember. After dialogues, ask them to repeat the dialogue with coursebooks closed, allowing them to improvise and change details.

**Try this** ☞ **One open, one closed**

Put students into A/B pairs. Allow Student A to open their coursebook but ask Student B to keep theirs closed. Ask Student A to describe a photo to Student B or, after both have completed a reading task, ask Student A to read the text aloud, stopping before certain words to see if Student B can remember what follows.

When students have their coursebooks open, our relationship with them can suffer. We may find ourselves having to tell them what exercise they should be looking at, or stopping them going on to the next task. This battle to direct their attention can make the teacher seem very controlling.

**✓ Getting it right** | **Books closed default**

Make sure that students close their coursebooks as soon as a particular activity has been completed. When you're ready to move on to another exercise, write the page and exercise number on the board and challenge each student to find it more quickly than their partner(s).

Of course there will be more opportunities to close the coursebook if teachers are selective about the content used. Dipping into content selectively will, in any case, help maintain students' interest.

**✓ Getting it right** | **Selecting content**

Use the coursebook as if it were a pool of potential resources rather than something to be followed. This will make your lessons seem less predictable.

Finally, to engage students successfully with the coursebook, it's important to allow them to respond to the material in personal and creative ways.

**Try this ☞** | **Adding emoji**

During reading tasks, encourage students to add emoji to the margins to show how they feel when reading. Afterwards they should explain their choices. For example, a text about an adventure in the Amazon might produce:
☺ I thought this river trip was cool because I love canoeing.

# Digital media

Materials that are not specifically created for learners can appeal to their desire to engage with the world beyond the classroom. Online materials are particularly appealing since they are often up to date and include stimulating videos, images, and recordings shared and discussed by millions of people around the world. They also give learners the chance to develop the 21st century skills of media/technology literacy, and so can make learning seem highly relevant.

Difficulties with lesson preparation or grading can be overcome to some extent by using semi-authentic materials that have been adapted for teaching purposes, such as those at www.breakingnewsenglish.com, or authentic materials that have been worked into lesson plans, e.g. those at http://lessonstream.org. Another solution is to use authentic materials to meet grammar and vocabulary teaching objectives rather than to develop comprehension skills, since we can then help students understand meaning using translation software while they listen or read.

**Try this ☞** | **Translation software**

Copy and paste a short text, such as a job advertisement or joke, into an online translation tool such as Google Translate. Then make a copy of the L1 translation for each student. Have them correct any mistakes that Google Translate made. Then, using an online gap-fill generator, follow the on-screen instructions to create a gap-fill exercise of the original English text. Ask students to add in the missing words using their L1 translations to help them, then check their answers against the original text.

Using authentic materials doesn't always involve using authentic texts. We can use visual media from the 'real world' – photos, art, picture books, or silent films – to establish contexts for language work, and we can then elicit language from students. This allows them to contribute their existing knowledge to lessons, and involves more conversation and interaction in class, helping motivation to flourish.

---

**Try this** ☞    **Silent films**

Use films that can be understood visually, like the delightful *French Roast* animations, *Mr Bean* videos, or clips from Aardman studio films. Write up events that happen in the film and ask students to order them. Then ask them to retell the story in the past tense. Alternatively, take screenshots while you watch. Insert the saved images into a Word document and ask students to add conversations in speech bubbles, or act out the scenes with words.

---

**Try this** ☞    **Game and video breaks**

It isn't necessary to dedicate a whole lesson to authentic material. We can use online material as short breaks for students to reward them for good work and/or to reinforce coursebook objectives. Let students who put the most effort into their classwork or homework choose a short YouTube video for the class to watch, or play an online game on the interactive whiteboard while others cheer them on. Or use games and videos to give students a five-minute break during a lesson or between writing activities. (Games can be selected from websites such as www.funny-games.co.uk.)

---

# Content-based language teaching (CBLT)

Content-based language teaching (CBLT) involves introducing a non-linguistic aim into a language lesson. We might make a non-linguistic challenge the main focus of the lesson, such as solving a picture quiz, or we might select an aim from the curricula of other subjects, such as understanding how hurricanes develop. We could even teach or review a whole section of the curriculum of another subject area in agreement with colleagues – an approach referred to as Content and Language Integrated Learning (CLIL). Many modern coursebooks contain a CBLT component, and the internet provides a vast range of materials.

The motivational value of this approach is clear: students can acquire information and skills that are relevant to other learning objectives or interests, making English classes more valuable. It also allows students who may not be very proficient in English to use their knowledge of other subjects, building their self-esteem and their enjoyment of the language.

A further advantage is that the content of other subjects can often be understood with the assistance of graphs, maps, diagrams, and, of course, infographics – highly visual presentations of information. Such resources aid comprehension and give students an immediate sense of achievement.

**Try this** ☞ **From infographic to paragraph**

Select a simple infographic. You might choose one showing the benefits of drinking water, such as Figure 8.1. Hide the headline for the infographic and elicit ideas from the students, e.g. *It is a good idea to drink water*. Then ask learners to choose the two or three pieces of information from the infographic that they find most interesting and write them as sentences beneath their picture, e.g. *1) There is 35g of sugar in fizzy drinks; 2) We need water to help us concentrate*; etc. Add linking words to form a paragraph.

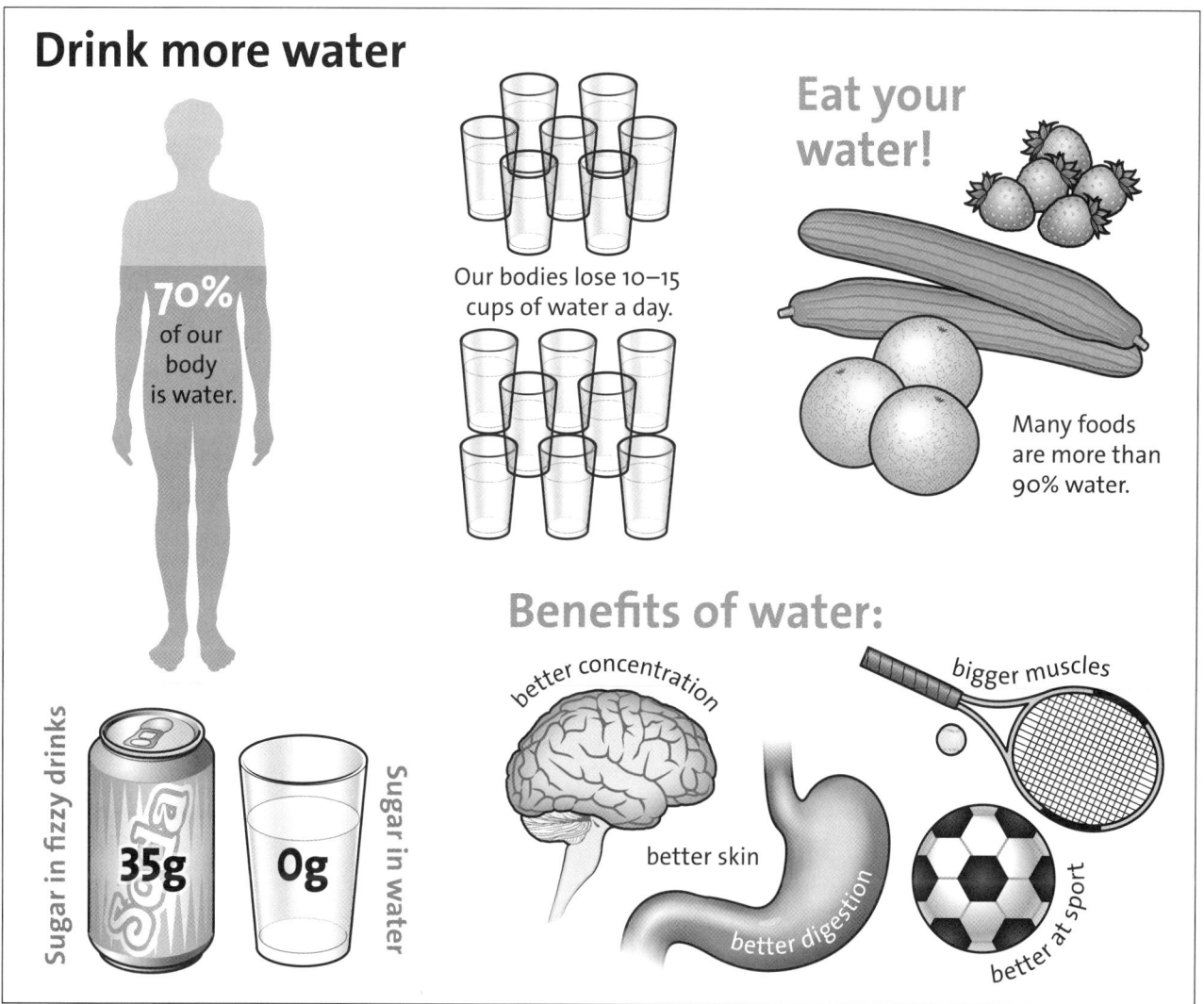

FIGURE 8.1    *Exploiting infographics for CBLT*

CBLT activities lend themselves particularly well to grammar lessons, as they often involve discussing cause and effect, comparison, or time relationships, all of which require particular features of grammar. When we describe the events on a timeline, for example, we provide students with an opportunity to use the past simple (*The Indian Ocean Tsunami took place in 2004.*), past perfect (*The euro had arrived by 2002.*), passive (*Facebook was created in 2004.*), time phrases (*Two years later …* ), and so on.

**Try this** ☞ **Timeline web quest**

Put up a timeline on the wall extending from the year your oldest student was born to the present day. Put students into pairs and give each pair a date from the timeline. Give them access to the internet (or they can use their own mobile devices if allowed) and have them find an event connected to each year. Students write up their findings on the timeline and present them to the class.

It's important to remember, however, that CBLT and digital resources will have greatest impact if used alongside regular course materials, to vary lesson content.

**Why this works** ➧ **Varying materials**

By using coursebooks in conjunction with a variety of materials, we allow students to benefit from the different sources of motivation that each offers. However, variety itself is also a source of motivation. Humans, like all animals, naturally seek out the new and unfamiliar. If we didn't, we wouldn't be able to do many things safely, such as driving. Our attention would be so absorbed by the familiar road surface that we'd miss the vital new information – a traffic light or street sign, for instance. Much about the learning environment doesn't change and students' interest will naturally decline over time. Input materials are one of the few things we can vary. Taking risks with the new may not always lead to successful learning, but it will help to keep your students interested.

# 9　Task design

Once we have created a stimulating environment and selected motivating materials for our students, we must ensure that motivation levels are sustained during lessons. It is largely the work the teacher has put into designing the tasks that will help achieve this. Whether we're designing short input tasks for the start of the lesson, or longer output tasks for the end, there are a few key factors to keep in mind.

## Creativity and skill

Providing an opportunity for learners to be creative with language is motivating, partly because it allows them to showcase their skills. The tasks teachers set in the early stages of language lessons are often designed to check understanding (e.g. to find, categorize, or match words), so they rarely allow much creativity, but there should always be room to introduce a little word play.

**Try this** ☞ **Word play**

Set some creative challenges to help students engage with input language. For example:
- expand a vocabulary set by adding students' own words
- place words from a sentence (or vocabulary set) into a crossword arrangement
- arrange the letters of a word into an anagram for their partner
- provide a substitute for each word in a sample sentence without changing the grammar.

The output tasks in later stages of lessons allow students to be more creative. We might ask them to write a dialogue or a letter, or tell a story, but these particular tasks are very language-centred and will appeal most to those with an intrinsic interest in English. Consider, by comparison, tasks in which the goal involves non-linguistic creativity. These might include activities which involve making or designing something – for example, practical tasks like wrapping a present, or the use of skills such as drama or problem-solving. Each of these can be performed using English, but they also give students the chance to use a range of additional knowledge and skills, and are meaningful beyond the language classroom. Engaging students' resourcefulness, particularly for tasks that are relevant to them, will increase their sense of **competence** and self-worth, thereby raising motivation.

Syllabuses typically require teachers to cover language by topic rather than task, and students may not often get a chance to engage in non-linguistic tasks through English. For this reason, we may want to organize lessons around a task from time to time.

**Try this** ☞   **Task-based lessons**

Select a 'real-world' task that will allow students to use language they have learnt. For example:

- planning a party (first conditional: *If we have it on Friday, people won't have homework.*)
- choosing a present from the internet (comparatives: *I think this smartphone is better.*)

Allow a couple of students to perform the task in their L1 first, while others listen. Stop them after two minutes and reflect on the language used. Explain that they are now going to do the task in English. Elicit useful structures they have recently studied. Students then create their own lists of target phrases which they tick off once they have been used.

Good coursebooks will feature creative tasks that include non-linguistic aims, and they may include additional resources that allow students to use a range of skills and knowledge.

✓ *Getting it right*   **Resource packs**

Look for good task-based activities in resource packs, which often contain a variety of extended tasks matched to teaching objectives. Pay special attention to those which feature some objectives that are non-linguistic in their outcomes, such as deciding how to spend money.

Listening and reading skills may seem to offer fewer opportunities for creative expression, but in fact there are many ways to engage with texts creatively.

**Try this** ☞   **Character interviews**

After reading or listening to a text, tell students to interview each other, with one taking on the role of one of the characters from the text and the other acting as a journalist looking for a good story. For example, after reading about the inventor John Logie Baird, they could ask questions like *Do you regret inventing the TV?* Allow them to record the interview and write a follow-up article.

**Try this** ☞   **Text adaptation**

Have students recreate a text. They could produce it in a different format. For instance, they might turn a dialogue into a monologue, or an audio recording into a play by adding stage directions and props. Alternatively, ask them to read the text to each other, changing some of the factual information. See how many false facts they can give without their partner noticing!

# Collaboration

One of the advantages of creative tasks is that they can be accomplished collectively. This is motivating because an individual's commitment to objectives is often greater when they are shared, and because group learning can satisfy social needs. Even tasks that are typically performed individually, such as writing, can be done in groups.

**Try this** ☞ **Group writing**

Break down a writing task into stages. For example, divide a biography into successive periods like infancy, childhood, and adolescence, etc. Ask students to write the first stage of the biography on a loose sheet of paper then fold it back to hide their writing. They then pass the paper to the person on their left, who writes the next stage, and so on.

Although it may seem more difficult to create tasks based on receptive skills, collaborative ELT materials frequently introduce 'jigsaw' reading/listening activities that require students to read and share information. Such activities can be improvised, especially if you have two texts, perhaps one from a coursebook and one from a workbook.

**Try this** ☞ **Jigsaw summarizing**

Sit students opposite each other at either side of a desk or table and give each a different text to read. Once they have finished, they should write each other's titles on a sheet of paper and interview each other in turn about their texts. Give them ten minutes to write summaries of their partner's text, encouraging them to add missing details. They then read each other's summaries and decide how accurate they are.

Another approach might be to provide different tools to members of a group. For example, one member could have the pen, another access to a text, and another a dictionary as they perform a reading or listening task. Alternatively we could have group members pool mental resources, as happens in many team games. Here, the idea is to set students a task that can't be easily accomplished individually but which becomes easier to do in a group (see page 55 for ideas on grouping students).

**Try this** ☞ **Key sentence dictation**

We often require students to find and underline sentences in texts containing target language. Instead of asking all students to do this, put them in A/B pairs and ask Student A to find and dictate the sentences for Student B to write down. For an added challenge, introduce a running dictation element by placing the books on tables around the edge of the room. Student A must then move between the book and their partner, memorizing the sentences. Make running dictation a group task by allowing a third person to be the spelling checker.

**Try this** ☞ **Paused listening**

Pause an audio recording halfway and ask groups to reconstruct the last sentence they heard. Ideally they should have one sheet of paper (or mini whiteboard) per group to encourage collaboration. The sentence should be between eight and 15 words long so that it's a little too challenging for individuals to remember. Give them the first word of each target sentence so they can clearly identify the sentence they need to reconstruct.

## Choice

Choice satisfies a learner's need for autonomy, and will therefore motivate. For example, our enthusiasm for reading a book increases if we've been allowed to select it, whereas it may drop considerably if someone chooses a book for us.

✓ *Getting it right*    **Setting output tasks**

Offer students as much choice as possible in creative tasks. Elicit suitable ideas from them (e.g. possible titles for creative writing homework, or names of bands they can review) and put them on the board. Have students take a photo of the options (or put up a photo yourself on the school Learning Management System).

In lessons where our objective is to develop general fluency in skills, it is fairly simple to offer choice.

✓ *Getting it right*    **Selecting readers**

When selecting class sets of readers, choose collections of short stories so that learners can decide on the story they'd like to read. They will then be able to share details of the story and make recommendations or write reviews for each other.

**Try this** ☞    **Presentations *X Factor***

Choose a website with a collection of video recordings of presentations, e.g. http://ed.ted.com. Ask students to vote for three presentation titles that appeal to them. Students watch two minutes of each video, and then rate the presentation according to criteria such as a) content, b) presenting style, and c) visuals. Play the winning video in full.

It is less easy to offer choice around vocabulary or grammar teaching objectives. Even if we can find two texts that provide examples of the target language, it requires more preparation time to offer both to students. However, packages offered by publishers usually allow us to offer some options, and we could also extend choice in the way task outcomes are presented.

**Try this** ☞    **Component options**

If there are features of the coursebook's accompanying workbook or website that mirror the coursebook units, allow your students to choose which they'd like to use. For example, there may be exercises in the coursebook and workbook that practise the same skill, e.g. skim reading.

**Try this** ☞    **Exercise choices**

Invite students to select which exercises they'd like to do from the coursebook's review pages or the workbook. After they've done these exercises, have them explain to someone who did a different exercise which part of the exercise was the most difficult/easiest and why, and how they succeeded in doing it.

**Try this** ☞ **Presentations of learning**

Encourage students to demonstrate their learning by presenting language in different ways. For example, in a vocabulary lesson students could show they've learnt ten words (chosen by you or them) by presenting examples of usage in a poster, an infographic, a story, an article, a vlog, a webpage, slides, a flipchart, or in any other way they like.

# Challenge

When beginning a new task, learners are likely to ask themselves, *Do we know what we're supposed to do? Is there a clear outcome? Can we finish it?* A student's enthusiasm for a task will depend on how clear the answers to these questions are. It's also important that students feel the level of challenge is right for them. Some will be drawn to difficult challenges, whereas others will shy away from them. Tasks must cater to both types of learner. One way of doing this is to break the task objectives down into varying degrees of difficulty. Teachers can do this before class, or ask students to select the level of challenge themselves.

**Try this** ☞ **Sequential targets**

When asking students to brainstorm ideas or spot differences, set a sequence of staged targets, making the value attached to each target clear by adding value 'tags' or eliciting them from students:
- two differences (*nice try! OK!*)
- four differences (*good work!*)
- six differences (*genius!*)

**Try this** ☞ **Choosing requirements**

When designing a task for students, create two options in which you vary the requirements: 'Let's play it safe' and 'I fancy a challenge'. For example, in a writing task, vary the number of adjectives and adverbs you ask for, the number of words, the amount of direct speech, or perhaps the number of characters. Alternatively, leave gaps in place of these variables in the instructions and ask students to add their own numbers.

**Try this** ☞ **Automatic gap-fill tests**

Allow students to create their own vocabulary/grammar tasks by copying and pasting text into an online gap-fill generator (see also page 69). These websites let students select the types of words they'd like to create gaps for (e.g. articles, modal verbs), the interval between gaps (e.g. every eighth word), or the level of the words they'd like to gap, thereby varying the challenge. If the tasks students create are too difficult, allow them to try again with different settings.

 **Getting it right**    **Feedback**

Make sure no task ends with the end-of-class bell. Challenging tasks will only be seen as worthwhile if time is given to recognizing achievement and praising students at the end.

## Control

Once we've extended a sense of control to students by giving them opportunities for choice, creativity, and independent target setting, we need to maintain it. As long as students find themselves waiting for external feedback during a task, they will not feel they are in complete control. What teachers aim to create in the classroom is a condition of **flow** – a state in which students are sufficiently engaged to become absorbed in a task. Flow is at its greatest when feedback is constant, or at least available when required.

**Getting it right**    **Teacher availability**

While students are doing tasks, make yourself available to them so that they can gain quick responses to their questions, but otherwise try to become as invisible as possible. Intervene only if you can see flow breaking down.

One of the barriers to achieving flow in productive tasks is the lack of feedback, especially where error correction is needed. In speaking tasks, students receive feedback by observing the reactions of their partners, but they don't get instant feedback in writing tasks, which can be frustrating and demotivating. There are two ways of addressing this problem. Either we can use technology that provides automatic feedback or we can set writing tasks that are so clearly structured that the need for corrective feedback is limited. Clear rules and guidelines will make it easier for learners to regulate their performance by themselves, or with support from peers (see Chapter 7 for ideas on peer-teaching).

**Try this** ☞    **Computer-assisted writing**

Allow students to write at computers so they can make use of auto-correction and editing tools to increase their sense of control during a writing activity. Some websites will allow students to copy in text they've written and provide scores and feedback directly. Investigate such websites online by searching for *computer-assisted instruction* or *computer-assisted writing*.

**Try this** ☞    **Guided production**

When doing writing tasks, provide students with a list of questions that will guide them sentence by sentence. For example, if they're drafting a story about a trip to the zoo, the initial questions could be:

1   When did you wake up? (I woke up at 7 a.m.)
2   What was the weather like? (It was sunny.)
3   How did you feel? (I felt excited.)
4   Where was Mum going to take you? (Mum was going to take me to the zoo.)

Ask students to write out their sentences, linking them with conjunctions. Allowing them to work in groups will enable students to support each other.

**Why this works** ⟶

> **Sustaining motivation**
>
> Researchers make the distinction between motivation *for* engagement and motivation *during* engagement. The point is that it's not sufficient to interest learners in a task; teachers must also encourage them to persist with the task. As we have seen, we can do this by ensuring that the tasks are challenging but controllable, and that they allow space for creativity, choice, and collaboration. However, it is often too late to introduce these elements once tasks have begun. Careful task design, then, is key to sustaining motivation.

# Part 3    Issues in motivation

# 10 Students as individuals

Though teachers may try to develop a style of teaching that is generally motivating, it's important to remember that learners will respond to certain motivation strategies differently, depending on factors such as their age, gender, personality, **aptitude**, and individual learning needs.

## Age

As learners move through the school system, their goals and priorities change. Children of primary school age tend to be motivated by the desire to participate and be accepted, especially by adults and older children. They appreciate opportunities to imitate grown-ups and receive praise from them, and so will find teacher-led group activities, in which they can demonstrate physical or language skills (e.g. chants, crafts, and games), very rewarding.

**Try this** ☞ **Vocabulary musical chairs**

If possible, arrange the chairs in the classroom in two rows, back to back. On every chair, put a flashcard for a recently learnt word. Have students move around the chairs to music and sit down when you stop it. Now ask students, *What are you sitting on?* They respond, *I'm sitting on a (lion)!*, etc.

**Try this** ☞ **Human letters**

Help students to learn spellings by having them make the shape of the letters with their bodies. Illustrate by writing a *W* on the board and (with your back to the students) arrange your body or arms into a 'W' shape. Put students into groups of six to nine and give them a day of the week to spell with their bodies.

As children approach early adolescence, their motivations change. Their priority becomes establishing themselves as individuals: they seek to distance themselves from adults who don't reflect back an identity they want to embrace, and will gravitate towards peers with strong identities they'd like to share. Therefore, flow (see page 78) will not be achieved easily unless students work within their chosen peer groups. For example, students may enjoy tasks where they can exercise their developing skills through group discussion.

**Try this** ☞ **Lateral thinking competition**

Put students in teams. Give each team a lateral thinking problem and (after they've had time to discuss it) the solution. For example:

Problem: A boy falls from the window of a 20-storey building and lives. How?
Solution: He fell from the ground-floor window.

Give out a sheet of paper with *all* the problems to each team. They discuss the solutions, checking their ideas for each one with the team who has the solution.

**Try this** ☞ **Quiz writing**

Assign different pages from the coursebook to students in teams and ask them to prepare a quiz based on the learning points. Insist that they use an agreed question format (e.g. five gap-fill questions with five options). Check and photocopy the quizzes. In the next lesson, give a copy of the quizzes to each team. Teams return their completed quizzes to the authors for marking. Authors award a point to the team for each correct answer and a point to themselves for each error.

✓ *Getting it right* | **Reduce teacher talk**

Teenagers may resent listening to explanations from teachers. Reduce teacher talking time and increase opportunities for peer-teaching.

## Grouping teens

Group identities have important implications for motivation. When students form their own groups, individual motivational characteristics can be reinforced as ambitious students, or those with low self-esteem, for example, attract each other. This means that the lack of motivation felt by some students may be intensified if we do not intervene. (See page 55 for ideas on handling friendship groups.) Activities that allow students to move between groups, or leave and return to groups, may help strike a balance between mixing students and allowing them to form groups freely.

**Try this** ☞ **Virtual chatrooms**

Tell students they are going to have conversations using sticky notes. Invite five or six volunteers to start by writing any comment they like on a sticky note and sticking it on the wall. Other students create 'threads' by writing a response on a new sticky note and adding it below others. Make sure contributions have a minimum length. If you give students different coloured sticky notes, you can introduce a sense of competition by seeing which colour group can make the most contributions.

The internet can also help us manage group work. Anonymous online groupings may allow students to benefit from peer work, without identity and personality issues becoming a problem. Online chats will also motivate teenagers, as they feel it is a familiar medium they can control and through which they can build their identity.

**Try this** ☞ **Computer-generated seating plans**

Students may feel resentful if the teacher always decides on their groups, so use computer software. Class Charts, for example, can either group or separate students according to points for poor behaviour, allowing teachers to avoid making unpopular decisions.

**Try this** ☞ **Online chat**

Try conducting discussion online, through websites such as https://todaysmeet.com. Create five or six chatrooms and distribute students randomly by giving each a number. Allow students to make up names to use in the chatrooms so that they can remain anonymous, but make sure you can match students to their online names in order to monitor inappropriate behaviour. You can enter the discussions too.

Naturally, as teenagers begin to suspect that their goals and interests are different from those of their teachers and parents/carers, they increasingly resent attempts to control them, and it is important for teachers to acknowledge this.

**Try this** ☞ **Negotiation**

Try making 'deals' with students. They should understand the logic that they have to do certain things in order to do others. Use humour to maintain good relationships and to avoid admitting that you have something planned which might seem boring: *I've prepared a really nice test for you ... (Groan.) What? You don't want to do my test? OK, let's make a deal. We'll do this for 20 minutes and then we'll watch a YouTube video. Does that sound OK?*

The move to secondary school brings further anxieties to teenagers. They suddenly find themselves among older students again, and among staff who are unaware of their backgrounds. Exams become increasingly important, and levels of reward in the environment drop as wall displays disappear and desks are arranged in rows. If we are to make sure these changes do not become barriers to motivation, we must stop students feeling exposed or threatened, especially during assessments.

**Try this** ☞ **Collaborative testing**

Allow students to work in teams for the second half of tests. Record an individual mark (a solo score) for the first part and a group mark (a team-work score) for the rest. Tell the class that you're equally interested in team-work scores, as these will indicate how good they are at collaboration.

## Gender and social roles

Differences between 'male' and 'female' minds may have been exaggerated in the past, but, as discussed in Chapter 2, motivation is influenced by our sense of who we are, which is affected by ideas of gender. Whether as a result of biology or identity, research suggests that male and female learners do differ, particularly in their response to failure. While male learners tend to attribute it to external factors (teachers, for example), female learners may see it as a reflection of their own ability. Female learners also report negative self-esteem and self-image problems more frequently, making them less likely to be assertive and participate in class. Low participation may result in fewer opportunities for attention and praise, a reduced sense of belonging, and difficulties in following classwork, thereby reducing performance levels and motivation.

**✓ Getting it right** **Participation**

Quiet students may look uncomfortable when speaking, but they'll probably prefer a chance to participate in class to being ignored. Invite them to speak out, even if they seem embarrassed and reluctant.

**Try this** ☞ **Delaying responses**

When asking a challenging question, write it on the board first and give students 30 seconds (or more if necessary) to write a one-sentence answer. Ask them to cover their answer and say it to the person next to them. Then invite shy students to share their answer with the whole class before asking more confident students.

In language learning, males may experience other threats to motivation. Research has suggested that they see learning languages as something girls are better at, and they therefore attach less value to it. Gender expectations increase as children age, and boys may at some point decide that their identity as males is better reinforced by doing subjects traditionally regarded as 'masculine', such as maths and sciences.

The view of language learning as somehow feminine may be connected to the notion that speaking is about relationship building and expression, perceived as more feminine characteristics. Teachers can challenge this perception by ensuring that language courses reflect a range of communicative purposes beyond relationship building.

✓ *Getting it right* | **English for specific purposes (ESP)**
Activities like negotiation, persuasion, or problem solving may appeal to students with traditionally 'masculine' interests. Look out for ESP materials that can be adapted to the general English classroom.

**Try this** ☞ | **Puzzle solving**
Use Sudoku puzzles in class to practise language of deduction and speculation. Put a puzzle on the board at the beginning or end of a lesson, labelling columns A–I and rows 1–9. Ask students to tell you what to do (*Put a 6 in E5.*) and to explain their reasoning (*It can't be a 5 because there's already one in that column, so it must be a 6.*). Invite students to solve further puzzles in groups.

# Aptitude

Many students lack motivation because they've come to believe that they have a low aptitude for language learning. This will happen when a student has greater difficulty with language tasks (e.g. memorizing word meanings, grasping patterns of word usage, or producing sounds) than their peers. The student will receive fewer rewards and less praise, and so may lose interest. They may also fear humiliation and withdraw effort in order to hide any lack of aptitude. Teachers can prevent this from happening by not giving out scores in class or using language that refers to ability when giving feedback.

✓ *Getting it right* | **Describing students**
Avoid phrases like *good at*, *intelligent*, and *able*, which describe qualities that students can't easily change. Students we don't describe in positive terms will quickly conclude that they aren't talented. Our comments should focus on progress, not qualities or standards.

**Try this** ☞ | **Strategy assessment**
When students submit a piece of work, assess them on their ability to identify strengths and weaknesses rather than giving a mark for the work itself. Read the work, highlighting mistakes and ticking things that work well, but don't add

grades or comments. Then have students list two things they did well and three they'll do differently next time. Score them one mark for a valid (but not key) point and two for identifying a key strength/strategy for improvement.

## Personality

Motivation for engaging in tasks will also depend on personality. Levels of alertness and responsiveness in class will be affected by several aspects of personality. Some degree of anxiety, for instance, can make learners more conscientious. Extroverts (outgoing types) can find it easier to put in effort, as they are more motivated by rewards. Teachers can engage impulsive and extroverted students by creating learning environments rich in rewards, such as social interaction, prizes, and even music.

 **✓ Getting it right**

**Stimulation**

Making lessons lively isn't always appropriate, as too much stimulation will prevent students from learning deeply. Try to use rewards and exposure only when needed to create an optimum level of alertness and responsiveness.

Another form of reward, particularly for extroverts, might come in the form of attention or exposure. Promise of a little exposure may also make slightly anxious learners raise their performance, and engage those who feel a degree of personal pride. Sharing work with others can therefore motivate students with a variety of personality traits.

 **✓ Getting it right**

**Recordings**

Making recording equipment available to students and having them produce sketches or podcasts for each other will motivate those who find sharing content with friends rewarding.

## Special educational needs (SEN)

Students with SEN often find classwork very frustrating. This may be particularly true for students with certain cognition and learning needs, since their relatively 'hidden' requirements can go unrecognized. However, students with other special needs, such as those with sensory impairments or interaction difficulties, may also find certain classroom activities less satisfying than their peers. If the time and space that students with SEN require to learn and contribute in class is not given, they will quickly develop a sense of low aptitude and low self-esteem, and withdraw from learning activities.

**Try this ☞**    **Key instructions**

Write out instructions on an individual whiteboard or laminated paper in the form of simple achievable steps and ask students to check off each one as they complete it. This will help them monitor their own progress.

Group games involving turn-taking provide the kinds of opportunities for structured participation and repetition which are particularly useful for students with SEN. In addition, we can use online media to extend opportunities for participation beyond normal lesson hours.

**Try this** ☞ **Discussion forums**

Allow students to use secure online discussion forums to contribute ideas in their own time. To boost their self-esteem, let them know you are looking forward to hearing their views.

Adaptations also need to be made to content and topics to make sure that learners are able to engage fully. Many students with SEN will be more motivated by opportunities to discuss personal interests and experiences, rather than abstract ideas, global issues, or distant futures. However, we can also learn from them about the activities they enjoy or would prefer to avoid.

**Try this** ☞ **SEN discussions**

Ask students if they would like to explain their SEN, either by giving a presentation or having a class discussion. Giving students the opportunity to talk about themselves can help promote understanding and build self-esteem.

✓ *Getting it right* **Learning from students**

Ask students with SEN how they like to learn – this will be useful information for you, and will also show the students that you value their individuality. Focus on issues that some students with SEN may be uncomfortable with, such as reading aloud, clapping out rhythms, dialogue work, or speaking about personal experiences.

Finally, it is essential to produce evidence of achievements in order to build a sense of competence and self-esteem. Make sure that students with SEN come away with clear achievements they can show to others at the end of a learning session.

**Try this** ☞ **Learning records**

Have students create a PowerPoint file for each lesson that they can store and show to others as a record of learning. It could contain an illustrated sentence per slide that showcases use of target language. A learning diary or portfolio (see page 34) may also be useful.

**Why this works** ‖‖▶ **Individual needs**

The degree to which a student will find the prospect of a lesson motivating will vary enormously from individual to individual. In fact, motivation in any one student may vary from day to day, and from morning to afternoon. Motivational teaching is therefore underpinned by sensitivity to, and understanding of, individual learner needs. For more ideas on motivating different types of learners, have a look at other books in the *Into the Classroom* series: *Special Educational Needs, Mixed-Ability Teaching,* and *Bringing creative teaching into the young learner classroom.*

# 11　Student background

The world beyond the classroom and our past experiences of education have an enormous impact on motivation. A learner's family and cultural background will inform their priorities and values, and previous learning experiences will influence their response to current learning environments. These factors, however, are perhaps the least visible to teachers and the least easy to control, as we may have little knowledge of students' experiences outside school. Remaining mindful of possible background issues allows teachers to make a contribution, however small, to managing them.

## Family background

It would be difficult to overstate the impact families have on student motivation. Consider first the way we are rewarded and punished as children. Students whose parents/carers always reward good behaviour may be unable to motivate themselves if a reward is not offered. A child who has received rewards too freely may not see effort as necessary at all and might place a low value on hard work in order to protect their self-esteem. If parents/carers think children should carry out responsibilities with no expectation of rewards, the child may have little motivation to put in effort.

**Try this** ☞ **Reflecting on effort**

Expecting constant effort may be unrealistic. Discuss when effort is most necessary and encourage students to use it in short, targeted bursts. For example, *We're going to try and memorize something, so I need five minutes of hard effort. Can you do that?*

Stability at home also has an impact on motivation. Stressful experiences in the family can make students more distracted and impulsive, and prevent them meeting learning goals. Young people may resent teachers for not knowing about their personal difficulties, and for expecting them to care about work.

**Try this** ☞ **Acknowledging feelings**

Acknowledging that students have lives and difficulties outside the classroom helps break down any resentment towards being in class. Allow students to rate their feelings at the beginning of class on a scale of 1–10, e.g. from '1 = rubbish' to '10 = totally cool' and discuss scores if they wish.

The way a young person relates to key figures in their life has a particularly strong influence on school relationships. A feeling of rejection by a parent/carer, for example, may lead to a general expectation of rejection, especially in adolescence, and a student may stop trying to please others through their efforts, or even test teachers to look for confirmation of their negative self-image.

✓ *Getting it right*

### Staying positive

Avoid falling into the trap of showing dislike for certain students. Engage with them and smile regardless of their behaviour. If you have to give a punishment, ask the student to tell you why, e.g. *James, I have to give you a detention. Can you tell me why?* Drawing attention to the rule will stop students from believing you dislike them.

Motivation may be negatively affected if families put too much pressure on children or if they panic about their child's performance in class, especially children at a young age. Children may become afraid to try, or feel they lack ownership of their learning. Making it clear that the classroom is a place where *students* get to make decisions can help them regain control.

Try this ☞

### Student-centred decisions

Encourage students to participate in classroom decision-making. Ask *Do you want a break now or in ten minutes?* or *How many questions do you think we need to practise?* Invite them to decide which materials (e.g. song lyrics or readers) are most useful for the class and to explain why.

Any student who has a weak relationship with parents/carers, for whatever reason, may see their relationship deteriorate further still when we give negative feedback about them, since we may strengthen negative perceptions that the parents/carers already have.

✓ *Getting it right*

### Positive notes on student records

Putting a positive note on a student record can help develop positive relationships between parents/carers and their children, and reduce stress in households with anxious adults. It can also strengthen a student's belief that their teacher is on 'their side'.

Try this ☞

### Self-esteem warmers

Build self-esteem with 'warmer' activities. For example, invite everyone to give a compliment to the person next to them. Alternatively, show images of self-confident people and ask students to imagine themselves in the bodies of those people. Tell them to sit like them, copy their expression, say what they're thinking, etc.

Family background may also affect a child's level of interest. If parents/carers do not engage their children in enriching activities, such as reading, or stimulate their interest and curiosity through discussion, there will be a narrower range of topics a child feels they can relate to. Lack of interest on the part of one student can easily spread to other class members, so taking time to tune students into topics is valuable.

Try this ☞

### Bridging interest gaps

Before studying a new topic, invite students to go online and find out about someone of their age who is interested in it. YouTube has many examples of young people who are passionate about gardening, astronomy, cookery, etc. Use their enthusiasm to engage students. Say, *I found three teenagers on YouTube who say they are interested in gardening. See if you can find them for homework.* In the next lesson, discuss why the three YouTubers seem interested.

✓ *Getting it right*

**Defending materials**

It's tempting for teachers to reflect our students' lack of interest in an attempt to get them on our side. We might say, *I know this is boring, but…*, which only confirms students' negative attitudes towards the subject. Try to express belief in your materials and plans.

**Try this** ☞   **Educational role models**

Show students pictures of role models who achieved both academically and in fields closer to students' hearts. (For example, footballer Edwin van der Sar got a master's degree.) Invite students to research the role models' educational background. This will help students understand that they needn't choose between education and other passions.

## Learning background

Most students who lack motivation to learn English point to the teacher as the main source of their demotivation. Students who have had poor learning experiences in the past may be more likely to label teaching as poor and to disengage. Good experiences can also be a demotivating factor if students miss previous teachers or peers who have left. Increasing the number of 'getting to know you' activities will help students bond with new peers and deal with the 'loss' of past relationships.

**Try this** ☞   **Experience questionnaires**

At the start of learning programmes, students commonly complete questionnaires which focus on future needs or expectations. Try including questions that allow students to refer to past experiences. This will help avoid triggers that weaken motivation. Questions you could include are: *What was your favourite activity in your last English class? Which learning activities did you hate doing?*

**Try this** ☞   **Sharing experiences**

Let students write and pass to you (anonymously) a slip of paper with a fact about themselves that they want to share (e.g. *I went to Disneyland last year.*). Write the facts on the board and invite the class to find the people they apply to by asking questions (*Did you go to Disneyland recently?*).

Another likely source of demotivation is experience of 'failure' in previous English classes. Students will not be motivated to participate in learning programmes if they expect to be a disappointment to teachers. It is important for students to know that our opinions of them will not depend on achievement.

**Try this** ☞ **Accepting failure**

Have students describe on a slip of paper a time when they failed to achieve something. Read each one out anonymously and react positively, e.g. *That's normal: it happened to me too.* Tell students that they will not be blamed for failure in your class, and that you will still like them.

Students who haven't been high achievers in the past may have built an identity around low attainment, since peers often pay attention to learners who don't perform well in their studies.

 *Getting it right* | **Reserving praise**

Be sensitive to students who don't wish to receive praise in front of peers. Look out for moments when they are alone before highlighting when they've been successful.

Past school experiences will also influence the kinds of activities students will engage with. For example, a background of rote learning may result in a reluctance to join in with communicative learning. We must support students if there are aspects of classroom practice they feel uncomfortable with.

✓ *Getting it right* | **Supported speaking**

Write up the language that students will need in order to perform a speaking task on the board, so that they can begin tasks by reading it. Then cover the language word by word to slowly reduce their reliance on it.

# Cultural background

The culture in the foreign language classroom can differ from the culture students are used to. Attitudes towards authority, gender roles, and modes of dress may all vary, as might the way we interpret visual images, music, or behaviour. Some students can therefore feel uncomfortable in language learning environments. While promoting interest in English-speaking cultures can motivate, teachers must make sure that students do not feel their culture is devalued, particularly if international media often portrays their countries in the context of problems. Activities that encourage cultural comparisons in a non-judgemental way promote inclusion. Search online for intercultural resource packs which are designed to raise awareness of cultural differences.

**Try this** ☞ **TV comparisons**

Show students extracts from two programmes in the same franchise (e.g. *X Factor*) or genre (soap operas, news, etc.) – one from an English-speaking culture and one from their own in their native language. Invite students to tell you about the programme from their culture and to highlight differences and similarities between the two extracts.

Students will engage more willingly with issues that are important in their culture. It is, for example, difficult to engage them in discussions about recycling or endangered species if these topics receive little attention in their local or national media.

✓ *Getting it right*   **Cross-cultural content**

Make sure materials reflect a variety of cultural attitudes, and avoid stereotypes and generalizations. Be especially careful with online content, which can be dominated by Western culture.

**Try this** ☞   **Translation into English**

Rather than using texts authored in English language contexts, have students use texts and stories from their own culture. You could ask them to retell a story, a poem, or song lyrics in English. Additionally, two students could act out greetings or gestures from their culture(s) while a third explains their meaning in English.

Cultural differences can also affect *how* students are motivated. For example, social goals, such as pleasing others, tend to motivate students from some cultures more than others. Similarly, students from individualistic cultures may respond more to competition.

✓ *Getting it right*   **Cultural sensitivities**

Be aware of your class's preference for cooperation or collaboration, and allow students the freedom to work alone, collaborate, or compete in teams if they prefer.

Some countries may generally place more value on career-building than others. Where education is seen as a step towards a career, students may value it as a way of impressing employers or university admissions staff.

✓ *Getting it right*   **Showcase portfolios**

Online portfolios of students' work (presentations, articles, stories, etc.) can be used as **showcase portfolios** that demonstrate their skills. This will help students see the relevance of their class work to their wider objectives.

Researchers have also pointed to the difference between cultures that value mastery of the skill itself and those that value measures of performance, i.e. results. Cultures where social comparison is linked to achievement will often focus on performance goals, and learners from these cultures may focus on exams and choose easier routes where available. Researchers believe that learners from a cultural background that values mastery tend to engage more with lessons, so we should focus on developing mastery orientation with all students, giving it greater emphasis in our teaching where it may be lacking.

**Try this** 👉 **Personal target sheets**

Create personal target sheets for homework assignments and stick them in the front of students' exercise books. As you mark their work, write a new target and check if previous targets have been met. Make space to allow for repeated attempts. This will help students focus on personal mastery and prevent comparison with others.

| Writing assignments | Attempt no. | Target for next assignment | Target met? |
| --- | --- | --- | --- |
| Writing about a friend | 1 | No errors with third person verbs | ✓ |
| Writing about a friend | 2 | Avoid writing 'nice' | ✓ |
| Writing about weekend | 1 | Don't repeat linking words | |

FIGURE 11.1 *Personal target sheets*

**Why this works** ⏩

**Understanding students' backgrounds**

Sociocultural theories of learning emphasize that learning takes place through interaction in specific cultural and social contexts. A learner's motivation to confront almost all tasks, such as reading, writing, or solving problems, will depend on their cultural and social significance, as will the standard learners hope to achieve when doing them. Researchers are keen to point out that, as individuals, we do not passively accept the cultural and social norms and standards that surround us. We may even try to reject them! Nevertheless, they form part of our learners' motivational 'landscape', and giving them due consideration will help us engage our students.

# 12 Teacher motivation

The degree to which teaching is motivational will depend on how motivated the teacher feels. Teachers who are happy with their workload, the courses they teach, and the level of support they receive will be more driven to motivate their students. As teachers, we may have limited control over our teaching environments, but if we are aware of the factors that influence our own motivation, we can help guide our managers.

## The school environment

In an ideal world, all schools would be designed to build motivation. Well-resourced spaces with warm, bright decor and rooms full of natural light would provide pleasant environments that lift mood and commitment levels. Open-plan learning spaces with glass walls and 'break out' areas for groups would make sure that an ethos of openness and collaboration surrounds staff and students, helping inspiration to flow.

Investment in school buildings and spaces is one of the key factors in motivation, but in reality, tight budgets and underinvestment mean most teachers have to lift mood and build collaboration within existing premises. Nevertheless, a programme of cosmetic changes and event planning can really help.

**Try this** ☞ **Mounted posters**

Suggest a photography competition entitled 'colour' and mount winning photographs in the school corridors. Staff and students should vote to decide the winner and add motivational quotations to encourage positive thinking in staff and students alike. For example, *Education is not the filling of a pail but the lighting of a fire* (W. B. Yeats). Make sure mounts can be changed or rotated to keep them looking fresh.

### Events

Special events often bring out the best in students and staff, and can help them relate to each other positively. It is very easy for cynicism and distrust to grow between staff and students in stressful educational environments, and celebrating common values can help prevent this. Charity events, in particular, can show colleagues and students the best in each other and produce a sense of pride in the group and trust in each other's motivations and intentions.

**Try this** ☞ **Hawaiian day**

Propose a day where teachers come into school wearing Hawaiian tops and sunglasses. Serve pineapple juice in the staff room. Encourage all staff to get involved – school management and administration, too!

**Try this** ☞ **Charity committee**

Suggest that the school sets up a charity committee involving staff and student representatives. You can organize sponsored events between staff and students, cake sales, auctions, and raffles. Hold stalls for each event in common areas. Raise money not just for the school but also for charities that staff and students care most about. Organize presentations on the struggle to extend education globally.

It's important to find opportunities for interaction across the school during instruction too. Limiting engagement to the classrooms can give students and teachers a sense of isolation and disengagement, removing the rewards that come from a sense of community. A sense that classroom activities are being witnessed beyond the classroom walls will help students regard lesson outcomes as having greater consequence.

**Try this** ☞ **Team teaching events**

Talk to colleagues in other departments about occasionally bringing classes together in large spaces. For example, English teachers could collaborate with history or geography staff to design a CBLT lesson involving worksheets and a treasure hunt to encourage students to move about and work together (see page 70).

**Try this** ☞ **Positive referrals**

Suggest the school provides a box outside or near the staffroom with slips of paper on which teachers can write students' names, classes, and reasons why they deserve praise. Nominated students can be called out of class and given a certificate of achievement. This will encourage the development of a positive learning ethos within the school.

# Staff development

The enthusiasm that many teachers demonstrate when they begin their career in education can easily be lost in the stress of daily teaching routines. A lack of variety in teaching routines is a particular problem. As we become familiar with lessons and materials, teaching can start to lose its vitality. A further issue is that teachers' sense of control will suffer when schools take the choice of materials or the design of curricula and schemes of work out of their control. Opportunities to observe colleagues teaching, be creative, experiment with ideas, and share them with one another will inspire teachers and ensure they do not lose their enthusiasm for teaching.

**Try this** ☞    **Material reviews**

Have a staffroom table where you collect new teaching materials and ideas from magazine articles and websites. Many websites feature free downloadable articles and materials, and perhaps your school could subscribe to an ELT magazine. Encourage your colleagues to try out these new ideas and post reviews on the school intranet or external website.

**Try this** ☞    **Delegate and report**

Suggest that all teachers in turn be allowed to attend conferences and training events, on the condition that they give a presentation when they come back on something that inspired them.

**Try this** ☞    **Sharing workshops**

Suggest holding fortnightly idea-sharing workshops where you and your colleagues demonstrate new ideas you have developed or tried, or bring inspirational articles you have read, and so on.

**Try this** ☞    **Uploading own materials**

Experiment with using your own materials in classes. If students like a particular kind of worksheet you create for them, start producing one regularly. Upload them to your own blog or to an ELT resource-sharing website.

As well as inspiring ourselves with new ideas and challenges within our workplaces, we also need to feel a sense of development and challenge in our careers. A sense of progression can be lacking in some educational jobs, but there are a range of opportunities for teachers wanting to get their names 'out there' and to embark on new adventures.

✓ *Getting it right*    **Career development**

Look for opportunities to present your ideas at conferences, and routinely submit articles to magazines. Video your lessons and post them online, or invite publishers and researchers you meet to come and observe you so that others can see your techniques. Propose local training events that you and guest speakers can lead.

Teachers can also gain a sense of authority and development simply from conducting their own research.

**Try this** ☞    **Action research**

Identify a problem in your classroom, such as lack of engagement. Take an idea designed to increase engagement, such as allowing students to talk in their L1 (see 'Encouraging imaginative thinking' on page 23). Think of a way of measuring any resulting change in student behaviour, e.g. measure the length of students' writing before and after implementing the idea. Publish the research on your blog.

## Evaluation practices

Summative (post-instruction) testing can put teachers in uncomfortable positions by making us play the role of supportive mentor during instruction, then critic and judge when we mark and report results. Poorly written or overly challenging tests may provoke students into blaming teachers (and vice versa), damaging our relationships with classes.

✓ *Getting it right*    **Test environments**

Where possible, suggest that a colleague invigilates when your students are doing an exam so that they don't associate your presence in the classroom with threatening experiences.

However, well-chosen summative assessments can help teachers to bond with their students. Learners may place a particularly high value on external, international exams, and working with them in the face of external challenges may increase group commitment. Exams that rate students (e.g. from A–E) may divide class members, but systems in which the class can work towards specific thresholds, especially if the level is carefully chosen to be achievable, can really unite them. Pass–fail tests with a large number of boundaries between levels are therefore ideal.

Internal exams with low pass thresholds can also enhance motivation. Breaking courses down into modules that students have to pass ensures that anxiety about final, high-stakes tests is reduced and that a sense of confidence and progress grows throughout the course. Adding a high 'distinction' band in each module will give stronger students something to aim for.

✓ *Getting it right*    **Managing failure**

Allow students who don't pass modular tests to have a second attempt. Many tests have two versions that will allow students to re-sit them. Report the results with 'pass'/'not yet' grades and explain how many percentage points students were away from their target grade, rather than telling them their score. Make sure that additional instruction (and even a short talk to restore confidence) is available to support those who don't pass.

Whether students are assessed through exam results, competitions, project work, or portfolios, make sure that their (and your) successes are celebrated by the school to add value to achievements. This will help teachers feel pride in their work too.

**Try this** ☞    **Award systems**

Suggest that an award system is implemented at your school, appropriate to the age of the students. Young learners may appreciate an 'award board' in the school corridor, where their photo and certificate can be displayed. Teenagers may appreciate the addition of points or credits to online profiles, allowing them to advance up online leader boards or earn privileges.

 **Getting it right**

**Balancing priorities**

Sometimes a school's priority is to report performance levels precisely and promptly, rather than to ensure students reach achievable targets. Be aware of conflicting priorities and, if possible, differentiate the way results are reported to students and management.

**Why this works** ▍▍▍➡

**Motivating teachers**

Research consistently emphasizes that there is nothing more likely to increase student motivation than a teacher who shows passion for what they do in the classroom. Such teachers spread enthusiasm amongst colleagues too. Finding ways to strengthen and rediscover both our love for our work and our confidence is perhaps the single most important step we can take towards becoming motivational teachers.

# Glossary

**Aptitude**  A natural ability to do something.

**Autonomy**  Freedom from external control.

**Behaviourism**  The idea that our behaviour is controlled by reward and punishment.

**Cognitive**  Relating to processing or gaining knowledge.

**Competence**  The ability to do something.

**Delaying gratification**  Resisting a small, immediate reward for a larger reward later.

**Demotivation**  A loss of motivation or lack of enthusiasm and/or interest in work.

**Esteem needs**  An individual's needs for respect, self-esteem, and self-confidence; to be accepted and valued by others.

**Expectancy**  Assessment of the likelihood of reward.

**First language (L1)**  The language that was acquired first in a person's life.

**Flow**  A feeling of being completely focused on an activity.

**Future self-guide**  Using a view of ourselves in the future to affect our thinking and behaviour now. See *'Ought to' self*.

**Instrumental motivation**  Behaviour driven by a desire to achieve something, such as getting a job or promotion.

**Integrative motivation**  Behaviour driven by a desire to belong to a community or group.

**Intrinsic motivation**  Behaviour driven by an interest or enjoyment of an activity.

**Learned helplessness**  A belief or assumption that a circumstance can't be improved upon, due to repeatedly negative past experiences.

**Learning goals**  Objectives designed to improve skills or knowledge. See *Performance goals*.

**Learning portfolio**  A tool for recording learning through evidence. See *Showcase portfolio*.

**Locus of control**  The extent to which an individual feels they can control events.

**Mastery**  A sense of gaining a comprehensive level of knowledge or skill.

**Mirroring**  The natural tendency to imitate someone else's behaviour.

**'Ought to' self**  An individual's sense of what is expected of them by, for example, their society, their culture, or their family. See *Future self-guides*.

**Performance goals**  Objectives to reach a specific level of skill. See *Learning goals*.

**Reward**  A feeling of pleasure or satisfaction gained from events, activities, or circumstances.

**Role model**  A person who is admired as an example to aspire to and imitated by others.

**Second language (L2)**  A language learnt after the first language (L1) has been acquired.

**Self-efficacy**  Confidence in one's ability to achieve or control something.

**Self-regulation**  The ability to guide one's thoughts and behaviours.

**Self-worth**  The extent to which we value and accept ourselves.

**Showcase portfolio**  A collection of work for demonstrating skill to others. See *Learning portfolio*.

**Stimulation**  A general level of activity or excitement in the brain.

**Student-centred** An approach to teaching that allows students to control learning processes.

**Temptation bundling** Transferring the positive associations of a pleasurable activity to a less pleasurable task by doing both at the same time.

**Token system** A system in which good behaviour is consistently recognized through specific rewards.

**Value** The degree of reward associated with a specific outcome.

# Useful websites

Explore resources from one of the foremost academics on motivation:
www.zoltandornyei.co.uk

Discover this approach to motivational target setting:
https://demandhighelt.wordpress.com

See what other teachers are doing. Click on the schools tab on this website and add other search terms (e.g. respect posters):
https://pinterest.com

Explore Carol Dweck's ideas on growth mindsets:
http://mindsetonline.com/whatisit/about

Explore Sugata Mitra's ideas on self-organized learning systems (soles):
www.theschoolinthecloud.org

Read interesting articles on motivation:
www.teachingenglish.org.uk/magazine/learner

Explore the range of motivational resources offered by OUP's Oxford Teachers' Club:
https://elt.oup.com/teachersclub

Find a selection of reliable academic research. (Go to 'resources' and then 'care, welfare and behaviour'):
http://www.eep.ac.uk

Explore this selection of further practical ideas:
www.dailyteachingtools.com/motivating-students.html